contents

The aroma of freshly baked bread and scones is one of life's pleasures, and a muffin laced with chocolate or fruit is pure temptation. The step-by-step techniques and helpful tips in this book will ensure that, in no time at all, you'll feel confident making even the most exotic breads. Our practical advice also takes the mystery out of scone- and muffin-making so that the lightest of scones and the most luscious muffins will be easy to bake.

Pamela Clark

Food Director

muffins

Muffins are simple to make and delicious eaten hot, warm or cold, with or without butter. They are best made on the day of serving. All of our mouth-watering recipes will make either 12 medium or 6 large muffins.

Evenly greased muffin pans should be slightly more than half-filled with mixture

To test if muffins are cooked, push a skewer into a muffin; when withdrawn, the skewer should be free from muffin mixture

☐ We used a medium-sized muffin pan (1/3 cup/80ml capacity), and a larger, Texas-style muffin pan (3/4 cup/180ml capacity). Other sized pans are available, but you will need to adjust baking times if you use these pans. Pans should be slightly more than half-filled with mixture, whatever size you use. Pans should be greased evenly or coated with non-stick spray.

☐ Butter should be firm from the refrigerator when it is to be chopped.

☐ Muffin mixtures require minimum mixing and should look coarse and lumpy. We found a large metal spoon or fork to be the best implement for mixing.

☐ Muffins are cooked when they are browned, risen, firm to touch and beginning to shrink from the sides of the pan. If in doubt, push a metal or wooden skewer into a muffin. When withdrawn, the skewer should be clean and free from muffin mixture. Turn muffins from the pan onto a wire rack as soon as they are baked to prevent them from becoming steamy. However, if muffins have a filling such as custard, caramel or jam, let them stand a few minutes before turning them onto a wire rack. These fillings can be extremely hot, so handle them carefully.

☐ Cold muffins freeze well; transfer to freezer wrap or freezer bags before freezing. Press bag gently or use a freezer pump to expel all the air. Correctly wrapped muffins can be frozen for up to 3 months.

☐ To thaw in a conventional oven, remove freezer wrap and re-wrap muffins individually in foil, place in a single layer on an oven tray in a moderate oven for about 20 minutes or until they reach the right eating temperature for you.

☐ Microwave ovens vary in power, so we can give only a general guide to thawing muffins this way. Remove freezer wrap from muffins, place in a single layer in the oven. Set the oven to DEFROST, MEDIUM LOW or 30%, according to your oven. Allow about 45 seconds for 1 muffin; 1 minute for 2 muffins; and 1 1/2 minutes for 4 muffins. Stand muffins for 10 to 15 seconds. Thawed muffins should not feel hot to the touch. If they feel hot, they are overheated. You may need to experiment for best results.

Note These recipes have not been tested to cook in a microwave oven.

the basic muffin recipe – easy as one, two, three...

2^1/$_2$ cups (375g) self-raising flour
90g butter, chopped
1 cup (220g) caster sugar
1^1/$_4$ cups (310ml) buttermilk
1 egg, lightly beaten

1 Grease 12 hole (^{1}/$_3$ cup/80ml capacity) muffin pan. Sift flour into large bowl, rub in butter.

2 Stir in sugar, buttermilk and egg. Do not over-mix; mixture should be lumpy.

3 Spoon mixture into prepared pan, bake in moderately hot oven 20 minutes.

MAKES 12

simple variations

fruit and spice

3 teaspoons mixed spice
1 cup (190g) mixed dried fruit

Sift spice with flour; add fruit with sugar.

date and orange

1 cup (160g) wholemeal self-raising flour
1^1/$_2$ cups (240g) seeded chopped dates
3 teaspoons grated orange rind

Substitute the wholemeal self-raising flour for 1 cup of the self-raising flour in basic muffin recipe. Add dates and rind with sugar.

choc chip and walnut

^{3}/$_4$ cup (140g) Choc Bits
1 cup (120g) chopped walnuts

Add Choc Bits and nuts with sugar.

date and orange; fruit and spice *(top tier)*
basic; choc chip and walnut *(bottom tier)*

banana maple muffins

You will need about 2 small (280g) over-ripe bananas for this recipe.

2 cups (300g) self-raising flour

¹/₃ cup (50g) plain flour

¹/₂ teaspoon bicarbonate of soda

¹/₂ cup (100g) firmly packed brown sugar

¹/₄ cup (60ml) maple-flavoured syrup

²/₃ cup mashed bananas

2 eggs, lightly beaten

1 cup (250ml) buttermilk

¹/₃ cup (80ml) vegetable oil

COCONUT TOPPING

15g butter

1 tablespoon maple-flavoured syrup

²/₃ cup (30g) flaked coconut

1 Grease 12 hole (¹/₃ cup/80ml capacity) muffin pan.

2 Sift dry ingredients into large bowl. Stir in maple syrup and banana, then eggs, buttermilk and oil.

3 Spoon mixture into prepared pan, sprinkle with coconut topping. Bake in moderately hot oven about 20 minutes.

Coconut Topping Melt butter in small pan, add maple syrup and coconut, stir constantly over high heat until coconut is lightly browned.

MAKES 12

chocolate hazelnut muffins

2^1/$_2$ cups (375g) self-raising
  flour
^{1}/$_2$ teaspoon bicarbonate
  of soda
^{1}/$_4$ cup (25g) cocoa powder
^{1}/$_2$ cup (100g) firmly packed
  brown sugar
125g butter, melted
2 eggs, lightly beaten
1 cup (250ml) buttermilk
1 cup (250ml) Nutella

1 Grease 12 hole (^{1}/$_3$ cup/80ml capacity) muffin pan.

2 Sift dry ingredients into large bowl, stir in butter, eggs and buttermilk.

3 Spoon one-third of the mixture into prepared pan, top with 1 level tablespoon of Nutella. Top with remaining mixture. Bake in moderately hot oven about 20 minutes.

MAKES 12

white chocolate and macadamia muffins

2 cups (300g) self-raising
   flour
2/3 cup (150g) caster sugar
3/4 cup (140g) White Bits
1/2 cup (75g) chopped
   macadamias, toasted
60g butter, melted
3/4 cup (180ml) milk
1 egg, lightly beaten

1 Grease 6 hole (3/4 cup/180ml capacity) muffin pan.

2 Sift dry ingredients into large bowl, stir in remaining ingredients.

3 Spoon mixture into prepared pan. Bake in moderately hot oven about 25 minutes.

MAKES 6

pear and pecan muffins

2¹/₂ cups (375g) self-raising
   flour

1 cup (125g) chopped pecans

1 teaspoon cracked black
   pepper

150g soft blue cheese,
   chopped

425g can pear halves in light
   syrup, drained, chopped

2 eggs, lightly beaten

¹/₂ cup (125ml) vegetable oil

¹/₂ cup (125ml) milk

1 Grease 12 hole (¹/₃ cup/80ml capacity) muffin pan.

2 Sift flour into large bowl, stir in nuts, pepper, cheese and pear, then
   eggs, oil and milk.

3 Spoon mixture into prepared pan, sprinkle with extra cracked pepper.
   Bake in moderately hot oven about 20 minutes.

MAKES 12

ginger date muffins with caramel sauce

1 cup (160g) seeded chopped dates

1/3 cup (80ml) water

1/4 teaspoon bicarbonate of soda

2 cups (300g) self-raising flour

1 cup (150g) plain flour

2 teaspoons ground ginger

1/2 teaspoon mixed spice

1 cup (200g) firmly packed brown sugar

2 teaspoons grated orange rind

1 egg, lightly beaten

1 1/4 cups (310ml) milk

1/4 cup (60ml) vegetable oil

CARAMEL SAUCE

1 cup (200g) firmly packed brown sugar

1 cup (250ml) cream

40g butter

1 Grease 12 hole (1/3 cup/80ml capacity) muffin pan. Combine dates and water in pan, bring to boil, remove from heat, add soda, stand 5 minutes.

2 Sift dry ingredients into large bowl, stir in date mixture and remaining ingredients.

3 Spoon mixture into prepared pan. Bake in moderately hot oven about 20 minutes. Serve warm muffins with caramel sauce.

Caramel Sauce Combine all ingredients in pan, stir over heat, without boiling, until sugar is dissolved, then simmer, without stirring, for about 3 minutes, or until thickened slightly.

MAKES 12

coffee hazelnut muffins

2 cups (300g) self-raising
  flour
³/4 cup (105g) plain flour
¹/3 cup (35g) packaged ground
  hazelnuts
1 cup (200g) firmly packed
  brown sugar
1¹/2 tablespoons coffee powder
1 tablespoon boiling water
2 tablespoons Nutella
2 eggs, lightly beaten
1¹/2 cups (375ml) buttermilk
³/4 cup (180ml) vegetable oil

HAZELNUT FROSTING

1 cup (160g) icing sugar mixture
1 tablespoon cocoa powder
2 tablespoons Nutella
40g butter, softened
1 tablespoon milk

1 Grease 12 hole (¹/3 cup/80ml capacity) muffin pan.

2 Sift flours into large bowl, stir in ground nuts and sugar, combined
  coffee and water, Nutella, eggs, buttermilk and oil.

3 Spoon mixture into prepared pan. Bake in moderately hot oven about
  20 minutes. Spread cold muffins with hazelnut frosting.

Hazelnut Frosting Sift icing sugar and cocoa into small bowl, stir in
remaining ingredients.

MAKES 12

cherry coconut muffins

**2 cups (300g) self-raising
  flour**
125g butter, chopped
1 cup (70g) shredded coconut
**1 cup (210g) red glace
  cherries, halved**
2/3 cup (150g) caster sugar
270ml can coconut milk
1 egg, lightly beaten

1 Grease 12 hole (1/3 cup/80ml capacity) muffin pan.

2 Sift flour into large bowl, rub in butter. Stir in remaining ingredients.

3 Spoon mixture into prepared pan. Bake in moderately hot oven about 20 minutes. Sprinkle with a little extra toasted shredded coconut and sifted icing sugar, if desired.

MAKES 12

coconut lemon syrup muffins

2 cups (300g) self-raising
   flour
90g butter
3/4 cup (165) caster sugar
1 cup (90g) coconut
1 tablespoon grated lemon rind
1 egg, lightly beaten
1 cup (250ml) coconut cream
2 tablespoons shredded
   coconut

LEMON SYRUP
1/2 cup (110g) caster sugar
1/4 cup (60ml) water
2 teaspoons grated lemon rind
1/4 cup (60ml) lemon juice

1 Grease 12 hole (1/3 cup/80ml capacity) muffin pan.

2 Sift flour into large bowl, rub in butter. Stir in sugar, coconut, rind, egg
   and coconut cream.

3 Spoon mixture into prepared pan, sprinkle with shredded coconut. Bake
   in moderately hot oven about 20 minutes. Pour hot lemon syrup over hot
   muffins, then turn onto wire rack to cool.

Lemon Syrup Combine all ingredients in pan, stir over heat, without
boiling, until sugar is dissolved, then simmer 2 minutes without stirring.

MAKES 12

marmalade almond muffins

2 cups (300g) self-raising flour
125g butter, chopped
1 cup (80g) flaked almonds
2/3 cup (150g) caster sugar
1 tablespoon grated orange rind
1/2 cup (125ml) orange marmalade
2 eggs, lightly beaten
1/2 cup (125ml) milk
1/4 cup (20g) flaked almonds, extra

1 Grease 12 hole (1/3 cup/80ml capacity) muffin pan.

2 Stir flour into large bowl, rub in butter. Stir in nuts, sugar and rind, then marmalade, eggs and milk.

3 Spoon mixture into prepared pan, sprinkle with extra nuts. Bake in moderately hot oven about 20 minutes.

MAKES 12

passionfruit, pineapple and mint muffins

You will need about 4 passionfruit for this recipe.

2 cups (300g) self-raising flour

125g butter, chopped

2/3 cup (150g) caster sugar

2 tablespoons chopped fresh mint

1/2 cup (115g) chopped glace pineapple

1/4 cup (60ml) passionfruit pulp

1/2 cup (125ml) cream

2 eggs, lightly beaten

YOGURT CREAM

1/2 cup (125ml) cream

1/2 cup (125ml) plain yogurt

1 teaspoon grated orange rind

1 tablespoon passionfruit pulp

1 Grease 12 hole (1/3 cup/80ml capacity) muffin pan.

2 Sift flour into large bowl, rub in butter. Stir in sugar, mint, pineapple, passionfruit pulp, cream and eggs.

3 Spoon mixture into prepared pan. Bake in moderately hot oven about 20 minutes. Serve muffins filled with yogurt cream.

Yogurt Cream Combine cream and yogurt in small bowl, beat with electric mixer until soft peaks form. Fold in rind and passionfruit pulp.

MAKES 12

blackberry streusel muffins

2 cups (300g) self-raising
  flour
1¹/₄ cups (170g) frozen
  blackberries
1 medium (150g) apple,
  peeled, coarsely grated
³/₄ cup (150g) firmly packed
  brown sugar
3 eggs, lightly beaten
¹/₃ cup (80ml) vegetable oil
¹/₃ cup (80ml) buttermilk

STREUSEL TOPPING

¹/₃ cup (50g) plain flour
2 tablespoons brown sugar
1 teaspoon mixed spice
30g butter

1 Grease 12 hole (¹/₃ cup/80ml capacity) muffin pan.

2 Sift flour into large bowl, stir in remaining ingredients.

3 Spoon mixture into prepared pan. Coarsely grate streusel topping over muffins. Bake in moderately hot oven about 20 minutes.

Streusel Topping Sift flour, sugar and spice into small bowl; rub in butter. Roll mixture into a ball, wrap in plastic wrap, freeze until firm enough to grate.

MAKES 12

choc honeycomb muffins

**2 cups (300g) self-raising
flour**

¹/₄ cup (55g) caster sugar

1 cup (190g) White Bits

**100g chocolate-coated
honeycomb, chopped**

1 egg, lightly beaten

60g butter, melted

1 cup (250ml) buttermilk

¹/₄ cup (60ml) honey

1 teaspoon vanilla essence

1 Grease 12 hole (¹/₃ cup/80ml capacity) muffin pan.

2 Sift flour and sugar into large bowl, stir in White Bits and honeycomb,
then remaining ingredients.

3 Spoon mixture into prepared pan. Bake in moderately hot oven about 20
minutes.

MAKES 12

citrus poppyseed muffins

125g soft butter

2 teaspoons grated lemon rind

2 teaspoons grated lime rind

2 teaspoons grated orange rind

2/3 cup (150g) caster sugar

2 eggs

**2 cups (300g) self-raising
flour**

1/2 cup (125ml) milk

2 tablespoons poppyseeds

1 Grease 12 hole (1/3 cup/80ml capacity) muffin pan.

2 Place butter, rinds, sugar, eggs, sifted flour and milk in medium bowl, beat with electric mixer until just combined, then beat on medium speed until mixture is just changed in colour; stir in poppyseeds.

3 Spoon mixture into prepared pan. Bake in moderately hot oven about 20 minutes.

MAKES 12

pineapple ginger muffins

2 cups (300g) self-raising
  flour

1 teaspoon ground ginger

125g butter, chopped

²/₃ cup (150g) caster sugar

1 cup (90g) coconut

¹/₂ cup (115g) chopped
  glace ginger

¹/₂ cup (115g) chopped
  glace pineapple

²/₃ cup (160ml) milk

2 eggs, lightly beaten

¹/₄ cup (60ml) golden syrup

GINGER CREAM

300ml thickened cream

3 teaspoons caster sugar

1 tablespoon finely chopped glace ginger

1 Grease 12 hole (¹/₃ cup/80ml capacity) muffin pan.

2 Sift flour and ground ginger into large bowl, rub in butter. Stir in sugar, coconut, glace ginger and pineapple, then milk, eggs and golden syrup.

3 Spoon mixture into prepared pan. Bake in moderately hot oven about 20 minutes. Serve with ginger cream.

Ginger Cream Beat cream and sugar together in small bowl until thick, stir in ginger.

MAKES 12

choc brownie muffins

2 cups (300g) self-raising flour

1/3 cup (35g) cocoa powder

1/3 cup (75g) caster sugar

60g butter, melted

1/2 cup (95g) Choc Bits

1/2 cup (75g) chopped pistachios

1/2 cup (125ml) Nutella

1 egg, lightly beaten

3/4 cup (180ml) milk

1/2 cup (125ml) sour cream

1 Grease 12 hole (1/3 cup/80ml capacity) muffin pan.

2 Sift dry ingredients into large bowl, stir in remaining ingredients.

3 Spoon mixture into prepared pan. Bake in moderately hot oven about 20 minutes.

MAKES 12

chocolate orange dessert muffins

2 cups (300g) self-raising
  flour

$^1/_2$ cup (50g) cocoa powder

$1^1/_4$ cups (275g) caster sugar

125g butter, melted

$^3/_4$ cup (180ml) buttermilk

1 egg, lightly beaten

2 tablespoons Grand Marnier

2 teaspoons grated orange rind

12 (120g) chocolate orange
  thins

CRÈME ANGLAISE

4 egg yolks

$^1/_2$ cup (110g) caster sugar

$1^2/_3$ cups (410ml) milk

1   Grease 12 hole ($^1/_3$ cup/80ml capacity) muffin pan.

2   Sift flour, cocoa and sugar into large bowl, stir in butter, buttermilk, egg, liqueur and rind.

3   Spoon mixture into prepared pan. Break each chocolate into 3 or 4 pieces, push chocolate into each muffin. Make sure that chocolate does not touch sides of muffin pan and that mixture almost covers the chocolate. Bake in moderately hot oven about 20 minutes. Serve muffins with crème anglaise.

Crème Anglaise Beat egg yolks and sugar in small bowl with electric mixer until thick and pale. Pour milk into small pan, bring to the boil, whisk milk into yolk mixture. Return mixture to pan, stir over heat, without boiling, until mixture thickens and coats back of spoon.

MAKES 12

apricot buttermilk muffins

1¹/₂ cups (225g) roughly chopped dried apricots

¹/₄ cup (60ml) brandy

3 cups (450g) self-raising flour

125g butter, chopped

¹/₂ cup (110g) caster sugar

2 eggs, lightly beaten

³/₄ cup (180ml) buttermilk

APRICOT BUTTER

60g butter

1 cup (160g) icing sugar mixture

1 tablespoon brandy

1 Grease 12 hole (¹/₃ cup/80ml capacity) muffin pan. Combine apricots and brandy in bowl, stand 20 minutes. Process apricot mixture until finely chopped, reserve ¹/₄ cup of apricot mixture.

2 Sift flour into large bowl, rub in butter. Stir in sugar, apricot mixture, eggs and buttermilk.

3 Spoon mixture into prepared pan. Bake in moderately hot oven about 20 minutes. Serve with apricot butter.

Apricot Butter Beat butter in small bowl with electric mixer until as white as possible. Gradually beat in icing sugar, brandy and reserved apricot mixture.

MAKES 12

banana date muffins

You will need about 2 large (460g) over-ripe bananas for this recipe.

**2 cups (300g) self-raising
   flour**
1 teaspoon mixed spice
**1/2 cup (100g) firmly packed
   brown sugar**
1 cup mashed bananas
**1 cup (160g) seeded
   chopped dates**
3 eggs, lightly beaten
1/3 cup (80ml) vegetable oil
1/3 cup (80ml) buttermilk

1 Grease 12 hole (1/3 cup/80ml capacity) muffin pan.

2 Sift dry ingredients into large bowl, stir in remaining ingredients.

3 Spoon mixture into prepared pan. Bake in moderately hot oven about
   20 minutes.

MAKES 12

rhubarb crumble muffins

2¹/₂ cups (375g) self-raising
  flour
²/₃ cup (130g) firmly packed
  brown sugar
100g butter, melted
1 cup (250ml) milk
1 egg, lightly beaten

FILLING

1¹/₂ cups (190g) chopped
  fresh rhubarb
¹/₄ cup (55g) caster sugar
2 tablespoons water
¹/₄ teaspoon grated lemon rind

CRUMBLE TOPPING

¹/₄ cup (35g) plain flour
¹/₃ cup (65g) firmly packed brown sugar
2 tablespoons toasted muesli
1 teaspoon grated lemon rind
30g butter, melted

1 Grease 12 hole (¹/₃ cup/80ml capacity) muffin pan.

2 Sift dry ingredients into large bowl, stir in remaining ingredients.

3 Half-fill prepared pan with muffin mixture, spoon filling into wells, top with remaining muffin mixture, spread carefully to cover filling. Sprinkle with crumble topping, press gently onto muffin mixture. Bake in moderately hot oven about 20 minutes.

Filling Combine all ingredients in small pan, bring to boil, simmer, uncovered, 5 minutes or until mixture is thick and rhubarb soft; cool.

Crumble Topping Combine all ingredients in small bowl; mix well.

MAKES 12

chocolate beetroot muffins

2 large (500g) beetroot

1³/₄ cups (260g) self-raising flour

¹/₃ cup (35g) cocoa powder

1 cup (220g) caster sugar

2 eggs, lightly beaten

¹/₃ cup (80ml) vegetable oil

¹/₃ cup (80ml) buttermilk

1 Grease 12 hole (¹/₃ cup/80ml capacity) muffin pan. Wash and trim beetroot, cut off leaves, leaving about 3cm stem attached. Boil, steam or microwave unpeeled beetroot until tender. Drain beetroot, rinse under cold water, drain. Peel beetroot while warm, blend or process until smooth. You need 1¹/₃ cups (330ml) beetroot puree.

2 Sift dry ingredients into large bowl, stir in beetroot and remaining ingredients.

3 Spoon mixture into prepared pan. Bake in moderately hot oven about 25 minutes.

MAKES 12

cranberry and camembert muffins

2 cups (300g) self-raising
  flour

2 tablespoons caster sugar

2 eggs, lightly beaten

1/3 cup (80ml) cranberry sauce

125g camembert cheese,
  finely chopped

1/2 cup plain yogurt

1/4 cup (60ml) milk

60g butter, melted

1/2 cup (125ml) cranberry
  sauce, extra

1/3 cup (40g) chopped walnuts

1 Grease 12 hole (1/3 cup/80ml capacity) muffin pan.

2 Sift dry ingredients into large bowl, stir in eggs, sauce, cheese, yogurt, milk and butter.

3 Half-fill prepared pan with mixture, make a well in each muffin, drop rounded teaspoons of extra sauce into each well, top with remaining muffin mixture. Sprinkle with nuts. Bake in moderately hot oven about 20 minutes.

MAKES 12

blueberry muffins

2 cups (300g) self-raising flour

³/4 cup (150g) firmly packed brown sugar

1 cup (150g) fresh or frozen blueberries

1 egg, lightly beaten

³/4 cup (180ml) buttermilk

¹/2 cup (125ml) vegetable oil

1 Grease 6 hole (³/4 cup/180ml capacity) muffin pan.

2 Sift dry ingredients into large bowl, stir in remaining ingredients.

3 Spoon mixture into prepared pan. Bake in moderately hot oven about 20 minutes.

MAKES 6

arrabbiata muffins

3 (120g) bacon rashers, finely chopped

2 cups (300g) self-raising flour

1 cup (150g) plain flour

$^1/_3$ cup (25g) coarsely grated fresh parmesan cheese

$^3/_4$ cup (90g) seeded sliced black olives

2 tablespoons shredded fresh basil leaves

1 tablespoon chopped fresh oregano

2 eggs, lightly beaten

2 tablespoons tomato puree

3 teaspoons sambal oelek

3 cloves garlic, crushed

$^3/_4$ cup (180ml) vegetable oil

1$^1/_2$ cups (375ml) buttermilk

1 tablespoon shredded fresh basil leaves, extra

1 Grease 12 hole ($^1/_3$ cup/80ml capacity) muffin pan. Cook bacon in heated pan until crisp, drain on absorbent paper, cool.

2 Sift flours into large bowl, stir in bacon, cheese, olives and herbs, then eggs, puree, sambal oelek, garlic, oil and buttermilk.

3 Spoon mixture into prepared pan, sprinkle with extra basil. Bake in moderately hot oven about 20 minutes.

MAKES 12

Arrabbiata
Muffins

roasted capsicum and fetta muffins

1 medium (200g) red capsicum

1 medium (200g) yellow
  capsicum

2¹/₂ cups (375g) self-raising
  flour

100g fetta cheese, chopped

¹/₂ cup (40g) grated fresh
  parmesan cheese

90g butter, melted

1 egg, lightly beaten

1 cup (250ml) milk

1 tablespoon chopped fresh
  rosemary

¹/₂ teaspoon ground black
  pepper

1 tablespoon sesame seeds

1 Grease 6 hole (³/₄ cup/180ml capacity) muffin pan. Quarter capsicums, remove seeds and membranes. Grill or roast both capsicums, skin side up, until skin blisters and blackens. Peel skin away, roughly chop capsicums.

2 Sift flour into large bowl, stir in capsicums, cheeses, butter, egg, milk, rosemary and black pepper.

3 Spoon mixture into prepared pan, sprinkle with seeds. Bake in moderately hot oven about 30 minutes.

MAKES 6

peppered zucchini and leek muffins

1 tablespoon olive oil

1 medium (350g) leek, sliced

3 small (270g) zucchini, grated

2 cloves garlic, crushed

2 cups (300g) self-raising
   flour

2 teaspoons curry powder

1 teaspoon ground coriander

1 teaspoon ground cumin

100g butter, chopped

1/2 cup (60g) grated tasty
   cheddar cheese

2 eggs, lightly beaten

1 cup (250ml) buttermilk

2 tablespoons olive oil, extra

TOPPING

3/4 cup (90g) grated tasty cheddar cheese

1 teaspoon cracked black pepper

1 teaspoon sea salt

1 Grease 12 hole (1/3 cup/80ml capacity) muffin pan. Heat oil in medium pan, add leek, zucchini and garlic, cook, stirring, until leek is soft and any liquid evaporated. Strain mixture, press out excess liquid; cool.

2 Sift flour, curry powder and spices into large bowl, rub in butter, stir in zucchini mixture and cheese, then eggs, buttermilk and extra oil.

3 Spoon mixture into prepared pan, sprinkle with topping. Bake in moderately hot oven about 20 minutes.

Topping Combine all ingredients in small bowl; mix well.

MAKES 12

chickpea and spinach muffins

¹/₄ cup (40g) cornmeal

1 tablespoon vegetable oil

4 green onions, chopped

2 cloves garlic, crushed

40 leaves English spinach,
  shredded

2 cups (300g) self-raising
  flour

1 cup (170g) cornmeal, extra

2 tablespoons finely chopped
  fresh basil leaves

1 egg, lightly beaten

1¹/₄ cups (310ml) milk

90g butter, melted

300g can chickpeas,
  rinsed, drained

2 tablespoons finely grated
  parmesan cheese

1 Grease 6 hole (³/₄ cup/180ml capacity) muffin pan. Sprinkle inside of pans with about half the cornmeal. Heat oil in medium pan, add onion and garlic, cook, stirring, until onion is just soft. Add spinach, cook, stirring, until spinach is just wilted; cool.

2 Sift flour and extra cornmeal into large bowl, stir in basil, egg, milk and butter, then spinach mixture and chickpeas.

3 Spoon mixture into prepared pan, sprinkle with cheese and remaining cornmeal. Bake in moderately hot oven about 25 minutes.

MAKES 6

spicy sausage and corn muffins

1³/₄ cups (260g) self-raising flour

1 teaspoon dried crushed chillies

¹/₂ teaspoon ground cumin

¹/₂ teaspoon ground coriander

1 teaspoon ground hot paprika

³/₄ cup (90g) coarsely grated smoked cheese

90g chorizo, chopped

¹/₂ medium (100g) red capsicum, chopped

¹/₂ medium (100g) green capsicum, chopped

1 clove garlic, crushed

1 small (80g) onion, grated

130g can creamed corn

2 eggs, lightly beaten

90g butter, melted

1 cup (250ml) buttermilk

¹/₂ teaspoon ground hot paprika, extra

1 Grease 6 hole (³/₄ cup/180ml capacity) muffin pan.

2 Sift flour into large bowl, add chillies, spices, cheese, chorizo and capsicums; mix well. Add garlic, onion and corn, then stir in eggs, butter and buttermilk.

3 Spoon mixture into prepared pan, sprinkle with extra paprika. Bake in moderately hot oven about 25 minutes.

MAKES 6

crusty onion and cheese muffins

1/4 cup (35g) plain flour

20g butter

1 teaspoon water,
approximately

1 tablespoon vegetable oil

1 medium (150g) onion,
halved, sliced

1 3/4 cups (260g) self-raising
flour

3/4 cup (110g) plain flour,
extra

3/4 cup (90g) grated tasty
cheddar cheese

1 tablespoon chopped
fresh chives

1 egg, lightly beaten

1 1/4 cups (310ml) buttermilk

1/2 cup (125ml) vegetable
oil, extra

CHIVE BUTTER

40g packaged cream cheese, softened

50g butter, softened

2 teaspoons lemon juice

1 tablespoon chopped fresh chives

1 Place plain flour into small bowl, rub in butter, mix in just enough water to bind ingredients. Press dough into a ball, cover, freeze about 30 minutes or until firm. Grease 6 hole (3/4 cup/180ml capacity) muffin pan. Heat oil in frying pan, add onion, cook, stirring, until soft and lightly browned; cool.

2 Sift self-raising and extra plain flour into large bowl, stir in half the onion, half the cheese and all the chives, then egg, buttermilk and extra oil.

3 Spoon mixture into prepared pan. Grate frozen dough into small bowl, quickly mix in remaining onion and cheese; sprinkle over muffins. Bake in moderately hot oven about 25 minutes. Serve with chive butter.

Chive Butter Beat cheese and butter together in a small bowl until smooth, stir in juice and chives.

MAKES 6

prosciutto, basil and tomato muffins

5 slices (75g) prosciutto

2¹/₂ cups (375g) self-raising flour

90g butter

1 egg, lightly beaten

1¹/₄ cups (310ml) buttermilk

¹/₃ cup (80ml) milk

¹/₃ cup (50g) drained chopped sun-dried tomatoes

2 tablespoons chopped fresh basil leaves

1 clove garlic, crushed

1 teaspoon cracked black pepper

1 tablespoon olive oil

1 Grease 6 hole (³/₄ cup/180ml capacity) muffin pan. Cut prosciutto into strips.

2 Sift flour into large bowl, rub in butter, stir in egg, buttermilk, milk, tomatoes, basil, garlic and pepper.

3 Spoon mixture into prepared pan, top with prosciutto, brush lightly with oil. Bake in moderately hot oven about 20 minutes. Cover with foil, bake a further 10 minutes.

MAKES 6

asparagus, salmon and mustard muffins

200g fresh asparagus
2¹/₂ cups (375g) self-raising flour
2 eggs, lightly beaten
1 cup (250ml) buttermilk
2 tablespoons Dijon mustard
125g butter, melted
100g smoked salmon, finely chopped

TOPPING
30g butter
¹/₄ cup (40g) chopped almonds
1 tablespoon finely grated parmesan cheese
1 teaspoon drained green peppercorns, crushed

1 Grease 12 hole (¹/₃ cup/80ml capacity) muffin pan. Snap off and discard tough ends of asparagus. Boil, steam or microwave asparagus until just tender. Drain, rinse under cold water, drain on absorbent paper; cool. Chop asparagus roughly.

2 Sift flour into large bowl, stir in eggs, buttermilk, mustard and butter, then asparagus and salmon.

3 Spoon mixture into prepared pan, sprinkle with topping. Bake in moderately hot oven about 20 minutes.

Topping Melt butter in small pan, add nuts, stir over heat until just beginning to brown. Stir in cheese and peppercorns.

MAKES 12

cheesy pizza muffins

1 small (150g) red capsicum

2¹/₂ cups (375g) self-raising
  flour

1 egg, lightly beaten

1¹/₄ cups (310ml) milk

¹/₃ cup (80ml) light olive oil

¹/₂ cup (60g) grated tasty
  cheddar cheese

¹/₄ cup (20g) grated fresh
  parmesan cheese

¹/₂ cup (60g) seeded black
  olives, halved

¹/₄ cup (35g) drained chopped
  sun-dried tomatoes

2 tablespoons chopped fresh
  basil leaves

2 teaspoons chopped fresh
  rosemary

¹/₄ cup (30g) grated tasty
  cheddar cheese, extra

1 Grease 6 hole (³/₄ cup/180ml capacity) muffin pan. Quarter capsicum, remove seeds and membranes. Grill capsicum, skin side up, until skin blisters and blackens. Peel skin away, cut capsicum into strips.

2 Sift flour into large bowl, stir in egg, milk, oil, cheeses, olives, tomatoes and herbs.

3 Spoon mixture into prepared pan, top with capsicum strips, sprinkle with extra cheese. Bake in moderately hot oven about 25 minutes.

MAKES 6

caramelised onions and polenta muffins

2 tablespoons olive oil

3 medium (450g) onions, sliced

1 teaspoon cumin seeds

1 teaspoon dried crushed chillies

2 tablespoons white vinegar

2 tablespoons caster sugar

3 cups (450g) self-raising flour

2 cups (340g) polenta

2 eggs, lightly beaten

185g butter, melted

1^1/$_3$ cups (330ml) milk

^{1}/$_4$ cup chopped fresh parsley

1 tablespoon chopped fresh thyme

1 Grease 12 hole (^{1}/$_3$ cup/80ml capacity) muffin pan. Heat oil in pan, add onions, seeds and chillies, cook, stirring, until onions are soft. Add vinegar and sugar, cook, stirring occasionally, about 20 minutes or until onions are golden brown; cool. Reserve ^{1}/$_4$ cup onion mixture.

2 Sift flour into large bowl, stir in onion mixture with remaining ingredients.

3 Spoon mixture into prepared pan. Bake in moderately hot oven 20 minutes. Serve muffins topped with reserved onion mixture.

MAKES 12

curried chicken muffins

1 tablespoon vegetable oil

1 small (80g) onion, finely
  chopped

3 (330g) chicken thigh fillets,
  finely chopped

2 tablespoons Madras curry
  paste

1 cup (250ml) plain yogurt

2¹/₄ cups (335g) self-raising
  flour

¹/₂ cup (125ml) vegetable
  oil, extra

2 eggs, lightly beaten

2 tablespoons lemon juice

2 tablespoons chopped fresh
  coriander leaves

ground hot paprika

1 Grease 12 hole (¹/₃ cup/80ml capacity) muffin pan. Heat oil in pan, add onion, cook, stirring, until onion is soft. Add chicken, cook, stirring, until chicken is just tender. Stir in curry paste, remove from heat, stir in yogurt; cool.

2 Sift flour into large bowl, stir in chicken mixture, extra oil, eggs, juice and coriander.

3 Spoon mixture into prepared pan, sprinkle with a little paprika. Bake in moderately hot oven about 20 minutes.

MAKES 12

ham and cheese muffins

2 cups (300g) self-raising
   flour
1/2 teaspoon chicken stock
   powder
1/2 teaspoon ground hot
   paprika
80g butter
6 slices (130g) ham, chopped
1¹/2 cups (185g) coarsely
   grated tasty cheddar cheese
1 egg, lightly beaten
1 cup (250ml) milk
ground hot paprika, extra

1 Grease 12 hole (¹/3 cup/80ml capacity) muffin pan.

2 Sift dry ingredients into large bowl, rub in butter. Stir in ham and
   cheese, then egg and milk.

3 Spoon mixture into prepared pan, sprinkle with a little extra paprika.
   Bake in moderately hot oven 20 minutes.

MAKES 12

breads

All of our delicious breads are made with step-by-step recipes. Some of these recipes use yeast, but even novice cooks shouldn't be deterred from using yeast. It is simply a raising or leavening agent. Baking powder is also used for leavening. Bread with no raising is known as "unleavened".

- ☐ You can use dry (dried) yeast or fresh compressed yeast. We use dry yeast packaged in 5 x 7g sachets (2 teaspoons per sachet). Bulk dry yeast is available in 500g or 1kg vacuum-sealed packs; it will keep in a cool, dry place for up to 1 year, if unopened. Store in the refrigerator in an airtight container after opening.

- ☐ Generally, 2 teaspoons (7g) of dry yeast is equivalent to 15g of compressed yeast, but it is a good idea to read and follow the instructions on the packet.

- ☐ Fresh compressed yeast has a limited shelf life and must be stored in the refrigerator in an airtight container.

- ☐ Liquid added to yeast should be warm, about 26°C. An easy "rule of thumb" method for those without a thermometer is to add $1/3$ boiling liquid to $2/3$ cold. If liquid is too cold, it will retard the yeast growth; if too hot, it will kill the action of the yeast.

- ☐ Gluten is important in bread-making, as it is the protein in flour which gives elasticity to the dough. However, if you are allergic to gluten, try our gluten-free bread.

Working on a floured surface, begin kneading by pressing the heel of one hand gently but firmly into the lump of dough and p-u-u-s-h it away from you

Proving is an important step in the bread-making process; place the kneaded dough in an oiled bowl, cover the bowl and stand it in a warm place until the dough has risen as specified

Kneading Kneading makes the dough smooth, pliable and elastic. Start by scraping the dough from the bowl onto a floured surface in front of you.

Now press the heel of one hand gently but firmly into the lump of dough and p-u-u-s-h it away from you. Lift the furthest edge of the dough a little, give the dough a quarter turn, fold the dough in half towards you, and repeat the press-and-push motion. Keep going for the time specified. When kneaded sufficiently, dough will spring back if pressed with a finger.

Proving An important step is proving the dough, or giving it time to rise after kneading. Place dough in an oiled bowl, turn dough lightly to grease top and prevent a skin forming. Cover bowl with a clean cloth or plastic wrap and stand it in a warm place away from draughts until dough has risen as specified.

Refrigerating retards proving. Place the kneaded dough, covered, in the refrigerator for up to 12 hours or until risen as specified.

Oven hints Always check the manufacturer's instructions for your oven. As a guide, the top of the bread should be in the centre of the oven; 220°C is the perfect temperature for baking bread. Sweet breads are baked at slightly lower temperatures. Cover bread loosely with foil if it is overbrowning.

To test if bread is cooked, tap bread firmly on the bottom crust with fingers; if it sounds hollow, it is cooked. You will need to turn the bread out of the pan into a tea-towel, tap quickly, and return to the pan for further baking, if necessary. Work with caution, as the bread will be very hot.

Note Recipes are unsuitable to microwave. See page 64 for freezing information.

basic white bread recipe

3 teaspoons (10g) dry yeast
¹/₂ cup (125ml) warm water
2 teaspoons sugar
2¹/₂ cups (375g) plain flour
1 teaspoon salt
30g butter, melted
¹/₂ cup (125ml) warm milk

1 Combine yeast, water and sugar in small bowl, whisk until yeast dissolves. Cover, stand in warm place about 10 minutes or until mixture is frothy.

2 Sift flour and salt into large bowl, stir in butter, milk and yeast mixture. Turn dough onto floured surface, knead 10 minutes or until dough is smooth and elastic.

3 Place dough into greased bowl, cover, stand in warm place about 1 hour or until mixture has doubled in size.

4 Turn dough onto floured surface, knead until smooth, roll dough to 18cm x 35cm rectangle, roll up from short side like a Swiss roll, place on greased oven tray, cut 4 diagonal slashes across top. Cover, stand in warm place about 20 minutes or until risen. Bake in moderately hot oven about 45 minutes. Turn bread onto wire rack to cool.

simple variations

brown bread

Substitute the wholemeal plain flour for half the plain flour. You may need to mix in a little more warm milk to make a firm dough.

french sticks

Starting at Step 4: Divide dough in half, shape each half into 40cm sausage, place onto 2 greased oven trays, cover, stand in warm place 15 minutes or until dough has risen. Cut slashes on bread sticks, sprinkle with tablespoon of plain flour. Bake in moderately hot oven about 20 minutes.

cottage loaf

Starting at Step 4: Shape dough into 20cm round, place onto greased oven tray, cover, stand in warm place 15 minutes or until risen. Cut slashes on bread, sprinkle with plain flour. Bake in moderately hot oven 30 minutes.

dinner rolls

Starting at Step 4: Divide dough into 12 portions, shape into rolls, place onto greased oven trays, cover, stand in warm place 15 minutes or until risen. Cut slashes on rolls, brush with milk, sprinkle with seeds, if desired. Bake in moderately hot oven about 20 minutes.

basic white bread loaf, cottage loaf, brown bread, french sticks, dinner rolls (clockwise from bottom left)

baps

2 teaspoons (7g) dry yeast
1 teaspoon sugar
$^1/_2$ cup (125ml) warm water
$^1/_2$ cup (125ml) warm milk
2$^1/_4$ cups (335g) plain flour
1 teaspoon salt
40g butter

1 Combine yeast, sugar, water and milk in small bowl, whisk until yeast is dissolved. Cover bowl, stand in warm place about 10 minutes or until mixture is frothy.

2 Sift flour and salt into large bowl, rub in butter. Stir in yeast mixture, mix to a soft dough. Turn dough onto floured surface, knead about 5 minutes or until smooth and elastic. Place dough in a large greased bowl, cover, stand in warm place about 1 hour or until dough has doubled in size.

3 Turn dough onto floured surface, knead until smooth, divide dough into 6 equal portions, knead into balls. Place balls about 5cm apart on floured oven tray. Dust lightly with a little extra sifted flour, cover with cloth. Stand in warm place about 10 minutes or until dough is well risen.

4 Dust balls again with a little more sifted flour, indent centres with a finger. Bake in hot oven about 15 minutes.

MAKES 6

olive bread with sage and oregano

4 teaspoons (14g) dry yeast

1 teaspoon sugar

1¼ cups (310ml) warm milk

1 cup (250ml) warm water

2 cups (300g) plain flour

⅓ cup (80ml) olive oil

3½ cups (525g) plain flour, extra

1 teaspoon salt

1¼ cups (150g) seeded black olives, halved

2 tablespoons shredded fresh sage leaves

2 tablespoons chopped fresh oregano

1 Combine yeast, sugar, milk and water in large bowl, whisk until yeast is dissolved. Whisk in sifted flour, cover, stand in warm place about 30 minutes or until mixture is doubled in size.

2 Stir in oil, then sifted extra flour and salt. Turn dough onto floured surface, knead about 10 minutes or until dough is smooth and elastic. Place dough in large greased bowl, cover, stand in warm place about 1 hour or until dough has doubled in size. Turn dough onto floured surface, knead in remaining ingredients.

3 Roll dough to 30cm x 35cm oval. Fold dough almost in half, transfer to large greased oven tray, shape dough into an oval. Cover dough, stand in warm place about 45 minutes or until dough has increased in size by half. Sift about another 2 tablespoons of flour over dough, bake in moderately hot oven about 45 minutes.

52

chapatis

Be aware that chapatis need to be cooked over a flame to achieve the blistered appearance.

1 cup (150g) white plain flour
1 cup (160g) wholemeal
  plain flour
1 teaspoon salt
20g ghee
³/₄ cup (180ml) warm water,
  approximately

1. Sift flours and salt into large bowl, rub in ghee. Add enough water to mix to a firm dough. Turn dough onto floured surface, knead about 10 minutes, working in about an extra ¹/₄ cup (35g) plain white flour. Cover dough with cloth, stand 1 hour. Divide dough into 14 portions. Roll portions on floured surface into 20cm rounds, cover with cloth, stand 10 minutes before cooking.

2. Heat griddle or heavy-based frying pan until very hot, cook 1 round at a time, for about 30 seconds on first side or until round just begins to colour; remove from pan.

3. Place uncooked side of chapati directly over medium flame, checking frequently until chapati begins to blister. Repeat with remaining rounds. Wrap cooked chapatis in a cloth to keep warm or serve while warm.

MAKES 14

roti

Dough can be made a day ahead and kept wrapped in refrigerator.

1 cup (150g) white plain flour

**1 cup (160g) wholemeal
  plain flour**

1 teaspoon salt

1 teaspoon ground coriander

1/2 teaspoon ground turmeric

2 teaspoons cumin seeds

1 tablespoon vegetable oil

**3/4 cup (180ml) water,
  approximately**

90g ghee, approximately

1 Sift flours, salt and ground spices into large bowl. Make a well in flour, add seeds, oil and enough water to mix to a soft dough. Turn dough onto floured surface, knead 10 minutes. Wrap dough in plastic, refrigerate 30 minutes.

2 Divide dough into 16 portions, roll each portion on floured surface to 16cm round.

3 Heat heavy-based frying pan until very hot, add about 1 teaspoon of the ghee, quickly turn pan to coat base with ghee. Place 1 round into pan, cook about 1 minute or until round is puffed slightly and bubbles start to form. Turn, brown other side. Repeat with remaining ghee and rounds. When ghee begins to burn in pan and a few roti have been cooked, wipe pan clean with absorbent paper.

MAKES 16

parathas with spicy potato filling

1 cup (160g) wholemeal plain flour
1 cup (150g) white plain flour
1/2 teaspoon salt
100g ghee, chopped
1/2 cup (125ml) water, approximately
100g ghee, extra

FILLING

1 large (300g) potato, chopped
1/2 small (125g) kumara, chopped
1 teaspoon coriander seeds, bruised
1/2 teaspoon ground cumin
1/4 teaspoon cayenne pepper
1/4 cup firmly packed fresh coriander leaves

1 Sift flours and salt into large bowl, rub in ghee. Stir in enough water to make ingredients cling together. Turn dough onto floured surface, knead about 10 minutes or until smooth.

2 Divide dough into 16 portions, roll each portion on floured surface into a 16cm round. Stack rounds between layers of plastic wrap to prevent drying out.

3 Divide filling among 8 rounds. Spread filling over rounds, leaving 7mm borders. Brush borders with water, top with remaining rounds, press edges together to seal.

4 Heat some of the extra ghee in large pan, add parathas in batches, cook until browned and slightly puffed on both sides; drain on absorbent paper. Repeat with remaining ghee and parathas.

Filling Boil, steam or microwave potato and kumara until tender. Mash vegetables coarsely, stir in spices and coriander.

MAKES 8

turkish bread

STARTER

1/2 teaspoon dry yeast

1/4 cup (60ml) warm water

2 tablespoons warm milk

1 cup (150g) plain flour

DOUGH

1 teaspoon dried yeast

11/2 cups (375ml) warm water

1 teaspoon sugar

3 cups (450g) plain flour

11/2 teaspoons salt

2 tablespoons olive oil

2 teaspoons sesame seeds

1 **Starter** Combine yeast, water and milk in small bowl, whisk until yeast is dissolved; stir in flour. Cover, stand in warm place for at least 6 hours or overnight.

2 **Dough** Combine yeast, water and sugar in small bowl, whisk until yeast is dissolved. Cover, stand in warm place about 10 minutes or until mixture is slightly foamy.

3 Turn starter onto floured surface, knead 2 minutes or until smooth. Cut starter into 2cm pieces. Sift flour and salt into large bowl, add yeast mixture, starter pieces and oil, mix to a soft dough. Turn dough onto floured surface, knead about 2 minutes or until almost smooth. Place dough into greased bowl, cover, stand in warm place about 40 minutes or until doubled in size. Turn dough onto floured surface, knead until smooth. Halve dough, knead each half for about 5 minutes or until smooth and elastic. Place each half of dough into greased bowl, cover, stand in warm place about 40 minutes or until almost doubled in size.

4 Roll each half of dough into an oval about 35cm long. Make indents evenly over dough with your finger; dust with a little flour, sprinkle with seeds. Cover dough with greased plastic wrap to prevent drying out while oven trays are being heated. Now place lightly greased oven trays in a very hot oven 3 minutes. Quickly remove plastic from dough, and quickly place dough onto hot trays. Bake in very hot oven about 12 minutes.

MAKES 2

cheese and bacon rolls

4 teaspoons (14g) dry yeast

1 teaspoon sugar

1¹/₂ cups (375ml) warm water

5 cups (750g) plain flour

2 teaspoons salt

¹/₂ cup (125ml) milk

2 tablespoons sugar, extra

60g butter, melted

1 egg, lightly beaten

1 tablespoon milk, extra

1¹/₄ cups (155g) grated tasty cheddar cheese

4 bacon rashers, finely chopped

1 Combine yeast, sugar and water in small bowl, whisk until yeast is dissolved. Cover bowl, stand in warm place about 10 minutes or until mixture is frothy.

2 Sift flour and salt into large bowl. Stir in yeast mixture, milk, extra sugar and butter, mix to a soft dough. Knead on floured surface about 5 minutes or until elastic. Place dough in greased bowl, cover; stand in warm place or until dough has risen.

3 Turn dough onto floured surface, knead until smooth. Divide dough into 16 portions, roll each to a 10cm x 12cm oval. Place onto greased oven trays, cover with greased plastic wrap, stand in warm place about 15 minutes or until dough has risen.

4 Remove plastic wrap. Brush rolls with combined egg and extra milk, sprinkle evenly with cheese and bacon. Bake in moderately hot oven about 20 minutes.

MAKES 16

spinach and fetta pizza

2 teaspoons (7g) dry yeast

1 teaspoon sugar

2¹/2 cups (375g) plain flour

1 cup (250ml) warm water

¹/2 teaspoon salt

2 tablespoons olive oil

¹/4 cup (40g) semolina

1 bunch (500g) English
spinach

10 (100g) cherry tomatoes,
halved

1 cup (200g) fetta cheese,
crumbled

¹/3 cup (25g) grated parmesan
cheese

TOMATO SAUCE

1 tablespoon olive oil

1 medium (150g) onion,
chopped

2 cloves garlic, crushed

425g can tomatoes

¹/2 cup (125ml) tomato paste

¹/4 cup chopped fresh basil
leaves

1 teaspoon sugar

1 Combine yeast, sugar, 1 tablespoon of the flour and water in small bowl, whisk until yeast is dissolved. Cover, stand in warm place about 10 minutes or until mixture is frothy. Combine remaining sifted flour and salt in processor, pour in combined yeast mixture and oil while motor is operating. Process until dough forms a ball. Turn dough onto floured surface, knead about 5 minutes or until dough is elastic. Place dough in large greased bowl, cover, stand in warm place about 1 hour or until dough has doubled in size. Turn dough onto surface sprinkled with half the semolina, knead 1 minute. Place dough on large oven tray sprinkled with remaining semolina; press dough into a 32cm square.

2 Boil, steam or microwave spinach until wilted. Drain spinach; chop finely. Spread pizza base with tomato sauce, leaving a 3cm border. Spread evenly with spinach, tomatoes and cheeses. Bake in very hot oven about 20 minutes.

Tomato Sauce Heat oil in pan, add onion and garlic, cook, stirring, until onion is soft. Stir in undrained crushed tomatoes, paste, basil and sugar, simmer, uncovered, about 5 minutes or until thickened.

mixed grain loaf

1/4 cup (50g) cracked buckwheat

1/2 cup (80g) burghul

1/4 cup (50g) kibbled rye

3 teaspoons (10g) dry yeast

1 teaspoon sugar

3/4 cup (180ml) warm milk

1/4 cup (60ml) warm water

21/4 cups (335g) white plain flour

1/2 cup (80g) wholemeal plain flour

1 teaspoon salt

1 tablespoon linseeds

2 teaspoons olive oil

1 egg yolk

1 teaspoon milk, extra

2 teaspoons sesame seeds

2 teaspoons cracked buckwheat, extra

1 Place buckwheat, burghul and kibbled rye in small heatproof bowl, cover with boiling water, cover, stand 30 minutes. Rinse well, drain well.

2 Combine yeast, sugar, milk and water in small bowl, whisk until yeast is dissolved. Cover, stand in warm place about 10 minutes or until mixture is frothy. Sift flours and salt into large bowl, add grain mixture and linseeds. Stir in oil and yeast mixture; mix to a soft dough. Turn dough onto floured surface, knead about 10 minutes or until dough is smooth and elastic. Place dough in large greased bowl, cover, stand in warm place about 1 hour or until dough has doubled in size.

3 Turn dough onto floured surface, knead until smooth. Divide dough into 3 pieces. Shape each piece into a 30cm sausage. Plait sausages, place into greased 14cm x 21cm loaf pan. Cover, stand in warm place about 30 minutes or until risen.

4 Brush dough with combined egg yolk and extra milk, sprinkle evenly with combined sesame seeds and extra buckwheat. Bake in moderately hot oven about 45 minutes.

gluten-free bread

3 cups (450g) gluten-free
  plain flour
1¼ cups (180g) buckwheat
  flour
2 teaspoons gluten-free
  baking powder
1½ teaspoons salt
1 cup (160g) sunflower
  seed kernels
70g butter, chopped
1½ cups (375ml) milk
2 eggs, lightly beaten
2 teaspoons poppy seeds

1 Sift flours, baking powder and salt into large bowl; stir in kernels.

2 Rub in butter; stir in combined milk and eggs; do not overmix.

3 Press mixture into greased 14cm x 21cm loaf pan; do not smooth top. Brush with a little extra milk, sprinkle with seeds. Bake in moderate oven about 1 hour. Stand bread 10 minutes before turning onto wire rack to cool.

pagnotta

2 teaspoons (7g) dry yeast
¹/₂ teaspoon sugar
¹/₂ cup (125ml) warm water
3¹/₂ cups (525g) plain flour
1 teaspoon salt
1 tablespoon olive oil
³/₄ cup (180ml) warm
water, extra
¹/₄ cup (60ml) warm milk,
approximately
1 teaspoon salt, extra

1 Combine yeast, sugar and water in small bowl, whisk until yeast is dissolved. Cover bowl, stand in warm place about 20 minutes or until mixture is frothy.

2 Sift flour and salt into large bowl, add yeast mixture, oil, extra water and enough milk to mix to a soft dough. Turn dough onto floured surface, knead about 2 minutes or until smooth. Place dough in oiled bowl, turn dough to coat all over with oil. Cover, stand in warm place about 30 minutes or until dough has doubled in size.

3 Turn dough onto floured surface, knead about 5 minutes or until smooth and elastic. Shape dough into a 58cm sausage, shape sausage into a ring on greased and floured oven tray, brush ends with water; press together gently. Place extra salt in small bowl, stir in 2 teaspoons of hot water. Brush dough with salt mixture, sprinkle with a little extra flour. Place in cold oven, turn temperature to moderately hot, bake about 40 minutes. Lift pagnotta onto wire rack to cool.

pumpernickel bread

2 teaspoons (7g) dry yeast
1 teaspoon sugar
1 cup (250ml) warm water
50g butter, melted
1 tablespoon molasses
1 tablespoon caraway seeds
1/2 cup (85g) cornmeal
1 1/2 cups (185g) rye flour
1 cup (150g) plain flour
2 tablespoons cocoa powder
1 teaspoon salt

1 Combine yeast, sugar and water in large bowl, whisk until yeast is dissolved; cover, stand in warm place about 10 minutes or until mixture is frothy. Stir in butter and molasses, then seeds, cornmeal and sifted flours, cocoa and salt. Turn dough onto floured surface, knead about 10 minutes or until smooth.

2 Place dough into greased bowl, cover, stand in warm place about 2 hours or until dough has doubled in size.

3 Grease 8cm x 26cm bar pan, line sides of pan with 2 layers of baking paper, extending 5cm above edge of pan. Turn dough onto floured surface, knead until smooth. Press dough into prepared pan. Cover loosely, stand in warm place about 45 minutes or until dough has risen to top of pan.

4 Cover pan with a sheet of foil. Bake in moderate oven 15 minutes, remove foil, bake about a further 30 minutes.

tips on freezing bread

- Large unbaked loaves are not satisfactory to freeze at home.
- Small breads such as dinner rolls, pizza bases and unglazed sweet buns are suitable to freeze if partly baked. Follow the recipe, but bake for only half the time, cool on the oven tray, then freeze, uncovered, on the tray until firm. Transfer to freezer wrap or freezer bags before storing in the freezer; press bag gently or use a freezer pump to expel all the air. Such products can be frozen for up to 3 months.
- To complete baking, thaw completely at room temperature and continue baking as specified in the recipe.
- To freeze baked loaves, cool bread as quickly as possible, pack in good-quality freezer bags, expel all air, and freeze as quickly as possible. It can be a good idea to slice the bread first so that you can take out just the amount you want. Correctly wrapped bread can be frozen for up to 3 months.

stollen

1¹/₄ cups (310ml) milk

1 teaspoon salt

¹/₂ cup (110g) caster sugar

2 teaspoons (7g) dry yeast

1 cup (150g) plain flour

3 cups (450g) plain
   flour, extra

160g butter, melted

2 eggs, lightly beaten

1 tablespoon grated lemon rind

¹/₄ cup (50g) glace cherries,
   chopped

¹/₄ cup (40g) raisins, chopped

¹/₄ cup (40g) mixed peel

2 rings (55g) glace pineapple,
   chopped

¹/₂ cup (80g) blanched
   almonds, chopped

¹/₂ teaspoon ground cinnamon

2 teaspoons caster sugar, extra

1 egg, lightly beaten, extra

1 Combine milk, salt and sugar in small pan, stir over heat until sugar is dissolved and milk warmed. Transfer to medium bowl. Whisk in yeast and sifted flour, cover, stand in warm place about 10 minutes or until mixture is frothy. Sift extra flour into large bowl. Stir in butter, eggs, rind, fruit, yeast mixture and nuts; mix to a soft dough.

2 Turn dough onto floured surface, knead about 5 minutes or until smooth and elastic. Halve dough, press each half into an 18cm x 25cm oval. Sprinkle with combined cinnamon and extra sugar, fold dough almost in half. Place stollens onto greased oven trays, cover with greased plastic wrap. Stand in warm place about 40 minutes or until stollens are risen slightly. Remove plastic wrap. Brush stollens with extra egg. Bake in moderately hot oven 10 minutes, reduce heat to moderate, bake about a further 15 minutes. Lift onto wire rack to cool.

MAKES 2

greek easter bread

2 teaspoons (7g) dry yeast

1 teaspoon caster sugar

3/4 cup (180ml) warm milk

1/2 cup (75g) plain flour

100g butter, melted

2 eggs, lightly beaten

**1/3 cup (75g) caster
  sugar, extra**

**3 cups (450g) plain
  flour, extra**

2 teaspoons ground aniseed

1/2 teaspoon salt

1 egg yolk

2 tablespoons milk, extra

1 Combine yeast, sugar and milk in large bowl, whisk until yeast is dissolved. Whisk in sifted flour, cover, stand in warm place about 45 minutes or until mixture has doubled in size. Whisk in butter, eggs and extra sugar. Stir in sifted extra flour, aniseed and salt in 2 batches. Turn dough onto floured surface, knead about 10 minutes or until smooth. Place dough in large greased bowl, cover, stand in warm place about 11/2 hours or until dough has doubled in size.

2 Turn dough onto floured surface, knead until smooth. Divide dough into 6 portions. Shape each portion into a 33cm sausage. Twist 2 sausages together; shape into a round. Repeat with remaining sausages. Place the 3 rounds close together on a lightly greased oven tray, brush joins with water, press rounds gently together.

3 Cover rounds, stand in warm place about 45 minutes or until risen. Brush rounds with combined yolk and extra milk, bake in moderately hot oven 10 minutes, reduce heat to moderate, bake about a further 30 minutes.

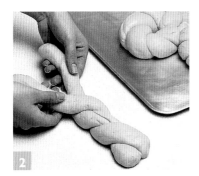

hot cross buns

4 teaspoons (14g) dry yeast
$1/4$ cup (55g) caster sugar
1 cup (250ml) warm milk
4 cups (600g) plain flour
1 teaspoon ground cinnamon
60g butter
1 egg, lightly beaten
$1/2$ cup (125ml) warm water
$3/4$ cup (110g) dried currants
$1/4$ cup (40g) mixed peel
1 tablespoon apricot jam

FLOUR PASTE

$1/2$ cup (75g) plain flour
1 tablespoon caster sugar
$1/3$ cup (80ml) water

1 Combine yeast, sugar and milk in small bowl, whisk until yeast is dissolved. Cover bowl, stand in warm place about 10 minutes or until mixture is frothy. Sift flour and cinnamon into large bowl, rub in butter. Stir in yeast mixture, egg, water and fruit, cover, stand in warm place about 1 hour or until mixture has doubled in size.

2 Turn dough onto floured surface, knead about 5 minutes or until smooth and elastic. Divide dough into 16 portions, knead into balls. Place buns into greased 23cm square slab cake pan, stand in warm place about 20 minutes or until dough has risen to top of pan.

3 Place flour paste into piping bag fitted with small plain tube, pipe crosses onto buns. Bake in moderately hot oven 10 minutes, reduce heat to moderate, bake about a further 15 minutes. Turn buns onto wire rack, brush with warm sieved jam.

Flour Paste Combine flour and sugar in small bowl, gradually blend in water, stir until smooth.

MAKES 16

chelsea buns

4 teaspoons (14g) dry yeast
1 teaspoon caster sugar
3³/₄ cups (560g) plain flour
1¹/₂ cups (375ml) warm milk
¹/₂ teaspoon ground cinnamon
¹/₄ teaspoon ground nutmeg
¹/₂ teaspoon mixed spice
2 teaspoons grated orange rind
1 tablespoon caster sugar, extra
1 egg, lightly beaten
45g butter, melted
15g butter, melted, extra
2 tablespoons raspberry jam
¹/₂ cup (75g) dried currants
¹/₄ cup (50g) brown sugar
¹/₂ cup (60g) chopped pecans, toasted
3 teaspoons honey

COFFEE ICING

1¹/₂ cups (240g) icing sugar mixture
15g butter, melted
2 tablespoons warm milk
3 teaspoons coffee powder

1 Combine yeast, caster sugar, 1 tablespoon of the flour and milk in small bowl, whisk until yeast is dissolved. Cover, stand in warm place about 10 minutes or until mixture is frothy. Combine remaining sifted flour, spices, rind and extra caster sugar in large bowl, stir in egg, butter and yeast mixture; mix to a soft dough. Turn dough onto floured surface, knead about 10 minutes or until elastic. Place dough in large greased bowl, cover, stand in warm place about 1 hour or until doubled in size.

2 Turn dough onto floured surface, knead 1 minute. Roll to a 23cm x 36cm rectangle. Brush dough with extra butter, spread with jam. Sprinkle with combined currants, brown sugar and nuts, leaving a 2cm border.

3 Roll dough up from long side, like a Swiss roll. Cut into 12 slices. Place slices, cut side up, in 2 greased 22cm round cake pans. Cover, stand in warm place about 30 minutes or until dough has risen slightly. Bake in moderately hot oven 30 minutes. Cool buns in pan 10 minutes, transfer to wire rack. Brush hot buns with honey, drizzle with coffee icing.

Coffee Icing Sift icing sugar into small bowl, stir in butter, milk and coffee, stir until smooth.

MAKES 2

panettone

¹/₂ **cup (85g) raisins**

¹/₄ **cup (40g) mixed peel**

¹/₂ **cup (80g) sultanas**

¹/₃ **cup (80ml) marsala**

8 **teaspoons (28g) dry yeast**

1 **teaspoon caster sugar**

¹/₄ **cup (60ml) warm milk**

5 **cups (750g) plain flour**

1 **teaspoon salt**

¹/₄ **cup (55g) caster sugar, extra**

3 **eggs, lightly beaten**

3 **egg yolks**

2 **teaspoons grated orange rind**

1 **teaspoon vanilla essence**

100g **butter, softened**

1 **cup (250ml) warm milk, extra**

1 **egg, lightly beaten, extra**

1 Grease 2 x deep 20cm round cake pans. Using string, tie a collar of greased foil around outside of prepared pans, bringing foil about 6cm above rims.

2 Combine fruit with marsala in small bowl; cover, stand 30 minutes. Combine yeast, sugar and milk in small bowl, whisk until yeast is dissolved. Cover bowl, stand in warm place about 10 minutes or until mixture is frothy.

3 Sift flour, salt and extra sugar into large bowl, make well in centre, add eggs and egg yolks, then rind, essence, butter, extra milk, yeast mixture and undrained fruit mixture.

4 Beat dough vigorously with a wooden spoon for about 5 minutes. This beating is important. The dough will be soft like a cake batter, and will become elastic and leave the side of the bowl. Cover bowl with greased plastic wrap, stand in warm place about 30 minutes or until dough has doubled in size. Remove plastic wrap. Turn dough onto floured surface, knead until smooth. Cut dough in half, knead each half on a well-floured surface for about 5 minutes or until the dough loses its stickiness. Press dough into prepared pans. Cover, stand in warm place about 30 minutes or until dough has doubled in size. Brush with extra egg. Bake in moderately hot oven about 15 minutes, reduce heat to moderate, bake a further 30 minutes.

MAKES 2

irish soda bread

2²/₃ cups (420g) wholemeal
plain flour

2¹/₂ cups (375g) white
plain flour

1 teaspoon salt

1 teaspoon bicarbonate of soda

2³/₄ cups (680ml) buttermilk,
approximately

1 Sift flours, salt and soda into large bowl. Stir in enough buttermilk to mix to a firm dough.

2 Turn dough onto floured surface, knead until just smooth. Shape dough into 20 cm round, place on greased oven tray.

3 Cut 1cm deep slashes in round in a cross shape, brush with a little milk. Bake in moderate oven about 50 minutes. Lift onto wire rack to cool.

onion focaccia

2 cups (300g) plain flour

1/2 teaspoon salt

2 teaspoons (7g) dry yeast

1/4 cup (20g) grated
parmesan cheese

1 tablespoon chopped
fresh rosemary

1 tablespoon chopped fresh
sage leaves

2 teaspoons chopped
fresh parsley

2 tablespoons olive oil

1 cup (250ml) warm water

1 small (80g) onion,
finely sliced

1 tablespoon sea salt

1 tablespoon olive oil, extra

1 Sift flour and salt into large
   bowl, stir in yeast, cheese and
   herbs. Pour in oil and water,
   gradually stir in flour; mix to a
   soft dough.

2 Turn dough onto floured surface,
   knead about 5 minutes or until
   dough is smooth and elastic.

3 Place dough on greased oven
   tray, press into 24cm round.
   Cover dough with greased plastic
   wrap, stand in warm place about
   1 hour or until doubled in size.

4 Remove plastic wrap. Sprinkle
   dough with onion and sea salt,
   drizzle with extra oil. Bake in
   hot oven about 25 minutes. Lift
   onto wire rack to cool.

kugelhupf

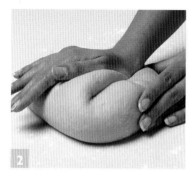

2 teaspoons (7g) dry yeast

1 teaspoon caster sugar

$^1/_2$ cup (125ml) warm milk

$^1/_2$ cup (75g) plain flour

150g butter

1 teaspoon vanilla essence

$^1/_2$ cup (110g) caster sugar, extra

$^1/_2$ teaspoon salt

3 eggs

3 cups (450g) plain flour, extra

WALNUT FILLING

30g butter, melted

1$^1/_2$ tablespoons warm milk

1 teaspoon coffee powder

$^3/_4$ cup (75g) finely chopped walnuts, toasted

$^1/_4$ cup (50g) brown sugar

2 teaspoons lemon rind

2 tablespoons stale breadcrumbs

1 teaspoon mixed spice

$^1/_2$ teaspoon ground ginger

1 Combine yeast, sugar and milk in large bowl, whisk until yeast is dissolved. Stir in flour, cover, stand in a warm place about 40 minutes or until mixture has doubled in size. Beat butter, essence, extra sugar and salt in small bowl with electric mixer until light and creamy, beat in eggs 1 at a time. Stir butter mixture and sifted extra flour into yeast mixture in 2 batches.

2 Turn dough onto floured surface, knead about 10 minutes or until smooth and elastic. Place dough in large greased bowl, cover, stand in warm place about 1$^1/_2$ hours or until doubled in size.

3 Turn dough onto floured surface, knead until smooth. Roll dough to 20cm x 40cm rectangle. Spread walnut filling over dough, roll up from long side as for Swiss roll. Brush 1 end of roll with water.

4 Grease and flour 21cm baba pan. Place roll in pan, seam towards centre of pan. Gently press dough into pan; press ends together to join. Cover pan, stand in warm place until dough is risen to within 1cm from rim of pan. Bake in moderately hot oven 10 minutes, reduce heat to moderate, bake about 40 minutes. Serve dusted with icing sugar, if desired.

Walnut Filling Combine butter, milk and coffee in small bowl; mix well. Stir in remaining ingredients.

pita bread

2 teaspoons (7g) dry yeast
1 teaspoon sugar
1¼ cups (310ml) warm milk
4¼ cups (635g) plain flour
1 teaspoon salt
½ cup (125ml) plain yogurt
1 egg, lightly beaten
¼ cup (60ml) water
1 tablespoon oil

1 Combine yeast, sugar and milk in small bowl, whisk until yeast is dissolved. Cover bowl, stand in warm place about 10 minutes or until mixture is frothy.

2 Sift flour and salt into large bowl. Stir in yeast mixture and combined yogurt, egg, water and oil. Turn dough onto floured surface, knead about 10 minutes or until smooth and elastic. Place dough in greased bowl, cover, stand in warm place about 1 hour or until doubled in size.

3 Turn dough onto floured surface, knead until smooth. Divide dough into 8 equal portions. Knead each portion into a ball, place onto lightly floured oven tray, cover, stand in warm place about 30 minutes or until risen.

4 Preheat oven to highest temperature. Roll each ball into a 25cm round. Heat an oven tray in a very hot oven, place 1 round at a time onto tray, bake in a very hot oven, on top shelf, for about 5 minutes or until bread is lightly browned and rounds begin to expand. Wrap cooked pita bread in a cloth to keep warm before serving.

MAKES 8

damper

3½ cups (525g) self-raising
  flour
1 teaspoon salt
2 teaspoons caster sugar
40g butter
½ cup (125ml) milk
1¼ cups (310ml) water,
  approximately

1 Sift flour, salt and sugar into large bowl, rub in butter. Stir in milk and enough water to mix to a sticky dough.

2 Turn dough onto floured surface, knead until just smooth. Place dough on greased oven tray, press into 16cm round.

3 Cut a cross in the dough, about 1cm deep. Brush dough with a little extra milk, then sprinkle with a little extra flour. Bake in moderately hot oven about 45 minutes. Lift onto wire rack to cool.

bagels

3 teaspoons (10g) dry yeast
1 tablespoon caster sugar
1/2 cup (125ml) warm water
1 cup (250ml) warm milk
3 cups (450g) plain flour
3 teaspoons salt
1 tablespoon caster sugar, extra
1 egg yolk
1 teaspoon water, extra
1 tablespoon poppy seeds
2 teaspoons sea salt

1 Combine yeast, sugar, water and milk in large bowl, whisk until yeast is dissolved. Cover bowl, stand in warm place about 10 minutes or until mixture is frothy. Stir sifted flour, salt and extra sugar into yeast mixture in 2 batches; mix to a firm dough.

2 Turn dough onto floured surface, knead about 10 minutes or until dough is smooth and elastic. Place dough into large greased bowl, cover, stand in warm place about 1 hour or until dough has doubled in size.

3 Turn dough onto floured surface, knead until smooth; divide dough into 12 portions. Knead each portion into a ball. Press finger in centre of each ball to make a hole, rotate ball with finger until the hole is one-third the size of the bagel. Place bagels about 3cm apart on greased oven trays, cover, stand in warm place about 15 minutes, or until risen.

4 Drop bagels individually into pan of boiling water; they must not touch. Turn bagels after 1 minute, boil further minute, remove with slotted spoon. Place bagels on greased oven trays. Brush tops with combined egg yolk and extra water, sprinkle with combined seeds and sea salt. Bake in moderately hot oven about 20 minutes. Cool on wire rack.

MAKES 12

brioche

4 teaspoons (14g) dry yeast

1/3 cup (80ml) warm water

1/4 cup (55g) caster sugar

4 cups (600g) plain flour

1 teaspoon salt

5 eggs, lightly beaten

250g butter

1 egg, lightly beaten, extra

1 tablespoon sugar

1 Combine yeast, water and 1 tablespoon of the caster sugar in small bowl, whisk until yeast is dissolved. Cover, stand in warm place about 10 minutes or until mixture is frothy. Sift flour, remaining caster sugar and salt into large bowl, add yeast mixture and eggs, stir until just combined. Turn dough onto floured surface, knead about 10 minutes or until dough is smooth and elastic.

2 Divide butter into 10 equal portions, knead each portion into dough, kneading well after each addition until all the butter is incorporated and dough is smooth and glossy. Place dough into large bowl, cover, refrigerate overnight.

3 Divide dough into 3 equal portions, shape into 45cm sausages. Place sausages onto large greased oven tray, plait sausages, cover, stand in cool place about 1 hour or until dough has nearly doubled in size. Brush plait with extra egg, sprinkle with sugar. Bake in moderately hot oven 10 minutes, reduce heat to moderate, bake a further 15 minutes.

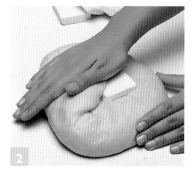

chilli corn bread

1 cup (150g) self-raising
   flour
1 teaspoon salt
1 cup (170g) cornmeal
1/2 cup (100g) kibbled rye
1 tablespoon brown sugar
1 teaspoon ground cumin
2 tablespoons chopped fresh
   parsley
1 teaspoon chopped fresh
   thyme
1/2 cup (60g) grated tasty
   cheddar cheese
310g can creamed corn
2/3 cup (90g) frozen corn
   kernels, thawed

2/3 cup (160ml) buttermilk
1/3 cup (80ml) milk
2 teaspoons sambal oelek
2 eggs, lightly beaten
50g butter, melted

1 Grease deep 19cm square cake pan, line base with baking paper. Sift
   flour and salt into large bowl, stir in cornmeal, rye, sugar, cumin, herbs
   and cheese.

2 Combine remaining ingredients in medium bowl; mix well, stir into dry
   ingredients.

3 Spread mixture into prepared pan, bake in moderately hot oven about
   1 hour. Stand, covered, 10 minutes before turning onto wire rack to cool.

fruit and nut loaf

2 teaspoons (7g) dry yeast

1/4 cup (55g) caster sugar

2 tablespoons warm water

2/3 cup (160ml) warm milk

1 cup (150g) plain flour

1 egg, lightly beaten

2 teaspoons grated orange rind

2 cups (300g) plain flour, extra

1 teaspoon salt

1/2 teaspoon ground cinnamon

100g butter, softened

1/4 cup (40g) sultanas

1/4 cup (40g) raisins

1/4 cup (35g) dried currants

1/4 cup (30g) chopped walnuts, toasted

1 egg yolk

1 tablespoon caster sugar, extra

1/2 teaspoon ground cinnamon, extra

1 Grease 14cm x 21cm loaf pan, line base with baking paper. Combine yeast, 2 teaspoons of the sugar and water in large bowl, whisk until yeast is dissolved. Whisk in milk and sifted flour. Cover, stand in warm place about 30 minutes or until mixture is frothy.

2 Stir in egg and rind, then sifted extra flour, salt, cinnamon and remaining sugar. Stir in butter, fruit and nuts.

3 Turn dough onto floured surface, knead until smooth. Place dough into greased bowl, cover, stand in warm place about 1 1/2 hours or until dough has doubled in size.

4 Turn dough onto floured surface, knead until smooth, place into prepared pan. Cover loosely with greased plastic wrap, stand in warm place about 30 minutes or until risen slightly. Remove plastic wrap. Brush dough with egg yolk, sprinkle with combined extra sugar and extra cinnamon. Bake in moderately hot oven 10 minutes, reduce heat to moderate, bake about a further 30 minutes. Turn onto wire rack to cool.

basic scone recipe

2¹/₂ cups (375g) self-raising flour
1 tablespoon caster sugar
¹/₄ teaspoon salt
30g butter
³/₄ cup (180ml) milk
¹/₂ cup (125ml) water, approximately

1 Grease a 23cm square slab cake pan. Sift flour, sugar and salt into large bowl, rub in butter with fingertips.

2 Use a knife to stir in milk and enough water to mix to a sticky dough.

3 Turn dough onto floured surface, knead quickly and lightly until smooth.

4 Use hand to press dough out evenly to 2cm thickness, cut into 5cm rounds. Gently knead scraps of dough together, and repeat pressing and cutting out of dough. Place rounds in prepared pan; brush with a little extra milk, if desired. Bake in very hot oven about 15 minutes.

simple variations

lemon and currant

1 quantity basic scone ingredients
¹/₂ cup dried currants
2 teaspoons grated lemon rind

Add currants and rind to flour mixture. Proceed as for basic scone method.

cumin seed and oregano

1 quantity basic scone ingredients
2 tablespoons chopped fresh oregano
3 teaspoons cumin seeds
2 teaspoons ground cumin
1 tablespoon tomato paste

Add oregano and cumin to flour mixture. Proceed as for basic scone method, combining paste with milk.

apricot wholemeal

¹/₂ cup (75g) chopped dried apricots
¹/₂ cup (125ml) boiling water
1¹/₂ cups (225g) white self-raising flour
1 cup (160g) wholemeal self-raising flour
1 tablespoon caster sugar
¹/₄ teaspoon salt
30g butter
³/₄ cup (180ml) milk, approximately

Place apricots in small heatproof bowl, pour over boiling water, stand 15 minutes or until cool. Proceed as for basic scone method. Add undrained apricot mixture after butter is rubbed into the flour, and enough milk to mix to a soft, sticky dough.

basic scones, lemon and currant, apricot wholemeal, cumin seed and oregano *(clockwise from top right)*

scones

Rise to the occasion with our easy-to-follow basic scone method, and you will soon see there's no mystery involved in making good scones. All these recipes have the same simple style, so you can progress to some delicious new combinations and choices. Scones are best made close to serving.

to make the perfect scone...

Make a soft, sticky dough
Most recipes give an approximate amount of liquid. This allows for the rate at which the flour absorbs liquid. The moisture content of the flour varies, depending on the flour's freshness and the weather. The dough must be soft and sticky and just hold its shape when turned out.

Use minimum flour when handling dough
Turn dough onto lightly floured surface, dust your hands with flour and shape the dough into a ball by working the dough gently into a manageable, smooth shape. This will give you smooth-topped scones. Avoid excess flour, which upsets the balance of ingredients and interferes with the overall browning.

Flatten the dough gently with your hand until it is an even thickness all over, press from the centre outwards. Use a floured, sharp metal cutter to cut as many scones as possible from the dough; these scones will be the lightest. Lightly knead the scraps together. Press dough out again slightly thicker to help make up for the second handling.

Bake at high temperatures
The oven temperature should be hot to very hot for good scones. They need to rise quickly to be light. Ovens vary greatly; always be guided by your own oven manufacturer's instructions for oven positions and temperatures. Usually, one test batch of scones in your oven will give you confidence to adjust time, temperature and oven positions. We prefer to cook scones close together in lightly greased, shallow aluminium cake pans. This method will give you straight scones with crusty tops and bottoms and soft sides. They need to be cooked slightly longer than scones on oven trays. If you prefer, cook scones on lightly greased oven trays, but only grease where the scones sit. If you like a scone crusty all over, space the scones about 1cm apart on the tray. If you like crusty tops and bottoms, place the scones just touching each other on the tray. They will support each other as they rise, but almost always some or all of the outside scones will topple and/or overcook.

Note Recipes are not suitable to microwave.

Cooling scones Always turn scones out of the pans or slide off oven trays onto wire racks. If you prefer crusty scones, cool the scones uncovered. To soften the crust, wrap hot scones in a clean tea-towel.

Glazing Glazing removes excess flour from the tops of scones and encourages them to brown. We use a brush dipped in water, milk or egg. Water results in a light brown, egg a golden brown, and milk is a good compromise. Glazing is not necessary.

To test scones are cooked Scones should be browned and sound hollow when tapped firmly on the top with your fingers. The scones in the middle are the ones to tap; they will take the longest to cook.

basic scone recipe

2¹/₂ cups (375g) self-raising flour

1 tablespoon caster sugar

¹/₄ teaspoon salt

30g butter

³/₄ cup (180ml) milk

¹/₂ cup (125ml) water, approximately

1 Grease a 23cm square slab cake pan. Sift flour, sugar and salt into large bowl, rub in butter with fingertips.

2 Use a knife to stir in milk and enough water to mix to a sticky dough.

3 Turn dough onto floured surface, knead quickly and lightly until smooth.

4 Use hand to press dough out evenly to 2cm thickness, cut into 5cm rounds. Gently knead scraps of dough together, and repeat pressing and cutting out of dough. Place rounds in prepared pan; brush with a little extra milk, if desired. Bake in very hot oven about 15 minutes.

simple variations

lemon and currant

1 quantity basic scone ingredients

¹/₂ cup dried currants

2 teaspoons grated lemon rind

Add currants and rind to flour mixture. Proceed as for basic scone method.

cumin seed and oregano

1 quantity basic scone ingredients

2 tablespoons chopped fresh oregano

3 teaspoons cumin seeds

2 teaspoons ground cumin

1 tablespoon tomato paste

Add oregano and cumin to flour mixture. Proceed as for basic scone method, combining paste with milk.

apricot wholemeal

¹/₂ cup (75g) chopped dried apricots

¹/₂ cup (125ml) boiling water

1¹/₂ cups (225g) white self-raising flour

1 cup (160g) wholemeal self-raising flour

1 tablespoon caster sugar

¹/₄ teaspoon salt

30g butter

³/₄ cup (180ml) milk, approximately

Place apricots in small heatproof bowl, pour over boiling water, stand 15 minutes or until cool. Proceed as for basic scone method. Add undrained apricot mixture after butter is rubbed into the flour, and enough milk to mix to a soft, sticky dough.

basic scones, lemon and currant, apricot wholemeal, cumin seed and oregano *(clockwise from top right)*

buttermilk scones

3 cups (450g) self-raising
   flour

1/4 teaspoon salt

1 teaspoon icing sugar mixture

60g butter

1³/4 cups (430ml) buttermilk,
   approximately

1 Grease 23cm square slab cake pan. Sift dry ingredients into large bowl, rub in butter, stir in enough buttermilk to mix to a soft, sticky dough.

2 Turn dough onto floured surface, knead until smooth. Press dough out to 2cm thickness, cut to 5.5cm rounds, place into prepared pan.

3 Bake in very hot oven about 15 minutes.

MAKES 16

spicy fruit scones

1¹/₄ cups (310ml) hot strong strained black tea

³/₄ cup (135g) mixed dried fruit

3 cups (450g) self-raising flour

1 teaspoon ground cinnamon

1 teaspoon mixed spice

2 tablespoons caster sugar

20g butter

¹/₂ cup (125ml) sour cream, approximately

1 Grease 23cm square slab cake pan. Combine tea and fruit in small heatproof bowl, cover, stand 20 minutes or until mixture is cold.

2 Sift dry ingredients into large bowl, rub in butter. Stir in fruit mixture and enough sour cream to mix to a soft, sticky dough.

3 Turn dough onto floured surface, knead until smooth. Press dough out to 2cm thickness, cut into 5.5cm rounds, place into prepared pan.

4 Bake in hot oven about 15 minutes.

MAKES 16

carrot banana scones

You will need 1 large (230g) over-ripe banana and 1 medium (120g) carrot for this recipe.

**2 cups (300g) white
self-raising flour**

**1/2 cup (80g) wholemeal
self-raising flour**

1/2 teaspoon ground cardamom

40g butter

**1/3 cup (65g) firmly packed
brown sugar**

1/2 cup mashed banana

1/3 cup finely grated carrot

**1/4 cup (30g) finely chopped
walnuts**

**1/4 cup (40g) finely chopped
raisins**

**3/4 cup (180ml) milk,
approximately**

ORANGE CREAM

50g packaged cream cheese, chopped

50g butter, chopped

1/2 teaspoon grated orange rind

1/2 cup (80g) icing sugar mixture

1 Grease 23cm round sandwich cake pan. Sift flours and cardamom into large bowl, rub in butter. Add sugar, banana, carrot, nuts and raisins, stir in enough milk to mix to a soft, sticky dough.

2 Turn dough onto floured surface, knead until smooth. Press dough out to 2cm thickness, cut into 5.5cm rounds, place into prepared pan.

3 Bake in very hot oven about 20 minutes. Serve with orange cream.

Orange Cream Beat cheese, butter and rind in small bowl with electric mixer until as white as possible. Gradually beat in sifted icing sugar.

MAKES 12

cardamom marmalade scones

2¹/₂ cups (375g) self-raising flour

1 teaspoon ground cardamom

30g butter

2 teaspoons grated orange rind

1 tablespoon caster sugar

¹/₃ cup (80ml) orange marmalade

1 cup (250ml) milk, approximately

MARMALADE BUTTER

125g butter

1 tablespoon orange marmalade

1 Grease 23cm square slab cake pan. Sift flour and cardamom into large bowl, rub in butter. Add rind, sugar and marmalade, stir in enough milk to mix to a soft, sticky dough.

2 Turn dough onto floured surface, knead until smooth. Press dough out to 2cm thickness, cut into 5cm rounds, place into prepared pan.

3 Bake in hot oven about 15 minutes. Serve with marmalade butter.

Marmalade Butter Beat butter in small bowl with electric mixer until as white as possible; stir in marmalade.

MAKES 16

caramel apple pull-apart

2 cups (300g) self-raising flour

30g butter

1 cup (250ml) milk, approximately

1/3 cup (65g) firmly packed brown sugar

410g can pie apples

pinch ground nutmeg

1/2 teaspoon ground cinnamon

1/4 cup (30g) chopped pecans, toasted

CARAMEL

1/4 cup (60ml) cream

20g butter

1/2 cup (100g) firmly packed brown sugar

1 Grease deep 22cm round cake pan. Sift flour into medium bowl, rub in butter, stir in enough milk to mix to a soft, sticky dough.

2 Turn dough onto floured surface, knead until smooth. Roll dough onto floured baking paper to 21cm x 40cm rectangle. Sprinkle dough with sugar, spread with combined apples and spices to within 3cm from long edge. Using paper as a guide, roll dough up like a Swiss roll. Use a floured, serrated knife to cut roll into 12 slices. Place 11 slices upright around edge of pan; place remaining slice in centre.

3 Bake pull-apart in moderately hot oven about 25 minutes. Stand a few minutes before turning onto wire rack to cool. Brush hot pull-apart evenly with caramel, sprinkle with nuts.

Caramel Combine all ingredients in small pan, stir constantly over heat, without boiling, until sugar is dissolved. Simmer, uncovered, without stirring, about 3 minutes or until mixture is thickened slightly.

golden honey muesli scones

**2 cups (300g) self-raising
flour**

1 teaspoon ground cinnamon

20g butter

1/2 cup (65g) toasted muesli

1/4 cup (60ml) honey

**3/4 cup (180ml) milk,
approximately**

1 tablespoon demerara sugar

1 Grease 20cm round sandwich cake pan. Sift flour and cinnamon into medium bowl, rub in butter, stir in muesli. Add honey, stir in enough milk to mix to a soft, sticky dough.

2 Turn dough onto floured surface, knead until smooth. Press dough out to 2cm thickness, cut into 5.5cm rounds. Place rounds into prepared pan, brush with a little extra milk, sprinkle with sugar.

3 Bake in very hot oven about 15 minutes.

MAKES 12

blueberry ginger scones with custard cream

2 cups (300g) self-raising
   flour
3 teaspoons ground ginger
1/4 cup (55g) caster sugar
50g butter
1/2 cup (75g) fresh or frozen
   blueberries
1/4 cup (60ml) sour cream
1/2 cup (125ml) milk,
   approximately

CUSTARD CREAM

1 cup (250ml) thickened cream
1/2 cup (125ml) thick custard
2 tablespoons icing sugar
   mixture

1 Grease 20cm round sandwich cake pan. Sift flour, ginger and sugar into medium bowl, rub in butter, add berries and sour cream. Stir in enough milk to mix to a soft, sticky dough.

2 Turn dough onto floured surface, knead until smooth. Press dough out to 2cm thickness, cut into 5cm rounds, place into prepared pan.

3 Bake in very hot oven about 15 minutes. Serve scones with custard cream, dusted with sifted icing sugar, if desired.

Custard Cream Beat cream, custard and sugar in small bowl with electric mixer until soft peaks form.

MAKES 12

honey wholemeal scones

**2 cups (300g) white
self-raising flour**

**1 cup (160g) wholemeal
self-raising flour**

1/2 teaspoon ground cinnamon

20g butter

1/4 cup (60ml) honey

**1 cup (250ml) milk,
approximately**

1 Grease 19cm x 29cm rectangular slice pan. Sift dry ingredients into medium bowl, rub in butter, stir in honey and enough milk to mix to a soft, sticky dough.

2 Turn dough onto floured surface, knead until smooth. Press dough out to 2cm thickness, cut into 5.5cm rounds, place into prepared pan.

3 Bake in hot oven about 20 minutes.

MAKES 15

glazed apricot almond scones

3 cups (450g) self-raising
   flour
1 teaspoon mixed spice
2 teaspoons caster sugar
30g butter
1 cup (150g) dried apricots,
   chopped
1/3 cup (45g) roughly
   chopped slivered
   almonds, toasted
1 egg, lightly beaten
11/4 cups (310ml) milk,
   approximately
2 tablespoons sieved
   apricot jam

1 Grease 23cm square slab pan. Sift flour, spice and sugar into large bowl, rub in butter. Add apricots and nuts, stir in egg and enough milk to mix to a soft, sticky dough.

2 Turn dough onto floured surface, knead until smooth. Press dough out to 3cm thickness, cut into 5.5cm rounds, place into prepared pan.

3 Bake in hot oven about 15 minutes, brush with jam.

MAKES 16

fruit and nut scrolls

If you prefer, you can use 1¹/₄ cups (380g) bottled fruit mince instead of the filling in this recipe.

3 cups (450g) self-raising flour
2 teaspoons caster sugar
50g butter
1¹/₃ cups (330ml) buttermilk, approximately

FILLING

¹/₄ cup (40g) sultanas
¹/₄ cup (35g) dried currants
¹/₄ cup (35g) chopped dried apricots
¹/₄ cup (50g) chopped seeded prunes
1 medium (150g) apple, peeled, finely chopped
2 tablespoons flaked almonds
2 teaspoons grated orange rind
2 tablespoons orange juice
¹/₃ teaspoon ground cloves
2 teaspoons rum or brandy
¹/₄ cup (50g) brown sugar

APRICOT GLAZE

2 tablespoons apricot jam
2 teaspoons water

ICING

¹/₃ cup (55g) icing sugar mixture
1 teaspoon hot water

1 Sift flour and sugar into large bowl, rub in butter. Stir in enough buttermilk to mix to a soft, sticky dough.

2 Turn dough onto floured surface, knead until smooth. Roll dough to 26cm x 36cm rectangle, spread with filling. Roll dough firmly from long side, like a Swiss roll. Cut roll into 2cm slices. Place slices, cut side up, about 3cm apart onto greased oven trays.

3 Bake in very hot oven about 15 minutes. Brush with hot apricot glaze, drizzle with icing.

Filling Combine all ingredients in medium bowl; mix well.

Apricot Glaze Combine jam and water in small pan, simmer few minutes or until glaze thickens slightly; strain.

Icing Combine icing sugar and water in small bowl, stir until smooth, pipe or drizzle over scrolls.

MAKES 18

zucchini gems with orange honey butter

Heat ungreased gem irons in hot oven for 5 minutes just before use; grease with cooking oil spray.

30g butter
²/₃ cup (150g) caster sugar
1 egg
1 small (90g) zucchini, finely grated
2 tablespoons dried currants
1¼ cups (185g) self-raising flour
pinch ground nutmeg
¹/₂ teaspoon ground cinnamon
¹/₄ cup (60ml) milk

ORANGE HONEY BUTTER

100g butter, softened
2 tablespoons grated orange rind
2 tablespoons orange marmalade
¹/₂ teaspoon mixed spice
2 tablespoons honey

1 Beat butter, sugar and egg in small bowl with electric mixer until just combined. Stir in zucchini and currants, then sifted flour and spices with milk in 2 batches.

2 Drop tablespoons of mixture into hot gem irons. Bake in hot oven 10 minutes. Turn onto wire rack. Serve warm gems with orange honey butter.

Orange Honey Butter Beat butter and rind in small bowl with electric mixer until smooth; stir in remaining ingredients.

MAKES 24

pistachio lime syrup gems

Heat ungreased gem irons in hot oven for 5 minutes just before use; grease with cooking oil spray.

30g butter

1 teaspoon grated lime rind

1/3 cup (75g) caster sugar

1 egg

11/4 cups (185g) self-raising flour

2/3 cup (160ml) milk

1/4 cup (35g) finely chopped pistachios

LIME SYRUP

2 tablespoons lime juice

2 tablespoons water

1/3 cup (75g) caster sugar

1 Beat butter, rind, sugar and egg in small bowl with electric mixer until combined. Stir in sifted flour and milk in 2 batches.

2 Drop tablespoons of mixture into prepared gem irons, sprinkle with nuts. Bake in moderately hot oven about 12 minutes. Turn onto wire rack, brush all over with hot lime syrup.

Lime Syrup Combine all ingredients in small pan, stir over heat, without boiling, until sugar is dissolved. Simmer, uncovered, without stirring, 2 minutes.

MAKES 24

bacon, egg and mustard scones

2 bacon rashers, finely chopped

2¹/₄ cups (335g) self-raising flour

90g butter, chopped

2 hard-boiled eggs, finely chopped

¹/₄ cup (20g) finely grated parmesan cheese

2 tablespoons chopped fresh chives

1 tablespoon seeded mustard

1 cup (250ml) milk, approximately

2 tablespoons finely grated parmesan cheese, extra

1 Grease 23cm round sandwich cake pan. Cook bacon in pan, stirring, until crisp; drain, cool.

2 Sift flour into medium bowl, rub in butter. Add bacon, eggs, cheese, chives and mustard, stir in enough milk to mix to a soft, sticky dough.

3 Turn dough onto floured surface, knead until smooth. Press dough out to 2cm thickness, cut into 5cm rounds. Place rounds into prepared pan, brush with a little extra milk, sprinkle with extra cheese.

4 Bake in very hot oven about 15 minutes.

MAKES 16

pesto swirls

3 cups (450g) self-raising
flour

1/4 teaspoon salt

90g butter, chopped

2 tablespoons chopped fresh
basil leaves

11/4 cups (310ml) milk,
approximately

2 tablespoons finely grated
parmesan cheese

FILLING

1/2 cup (100g) ricotta cheese

1/2 cup (40g) coarsely grated parmesan cheese

1/3 cup (80ml) bottled pesto

1/4 cup (40g) pine nuts, toasted

1/4 cup (35g) sun-dried tomatoes in oil, drained, chopped

1 clove garlic, crushed

1 teaspoon seasoned pepper

1 Sift flour and salt into large bowl, rub in butter. Add basil, stir in enough milk to mix to a soft, sticky dough.

2 Turn dough onto floured surface, knead until smooth. Roll dough to 25cm x 40cm rectangle, spread with filling. Roll up from long side, like a Swiss roll. Cut roll into 16 slices. Place slices, cut side up, about 3cm apart onto greased oven trays. Sprinkle with cheese.

3 Bake in moderately hot oven about 15 minutes.

Filling Combine all ingredients in bowl.

MAKES 16

sage pastrami scones

**1¹/₂ cups (225g) white
self-raising flour**
**¹/₂ cup (80g) wholemeal
self-raising flour**
15g butter
**2 tablespoons chopped fresh
sage leaves**
60g pastrami, chopped
**1 cup (250ml) milk,
approximately**

1 Grease 20cm round sandwich cake pan. Sift flours into medium bowl, rub in butter; stir in sage and pastrami. Stir in enough milk to mix to a soft, sticky dough.

2 Turn dough onto floured surface, knead until smooth. Press dough out to 2cm thickness, cut into 5cm rounds, place into prepared pan.

3 Bake in hot oven about 20 minutes.

MAKES 12

smoked salmon and sour cream scones

2 cups (300g) self-raising
  flour
150g smoked salmon, chopped
1/3 cup chopped fresh dill tips
1/4 teaspoon ground black
  pepper
1/3 cup (80ml) sour cream
1 cup (250ml) buttermilk,
  approximately

DILL CREAM

1/2 cup (125ml) sour cream
1/4 cup chopped fresh dill tips

1 Grease 19cm x 29cm rectangular slice pan. Sift flour into medium bowl, stir in salmon, dill and pepper, then sour cream and enough buttermilk to mix to a soft, sticky dough.

2 Turn dough onto floured surface, knead until smooth, press dough out to 2cm thickness, cut into 5.5cm rounds, place into prepared pan.

3 Bake in very hot oven about 15 minutes. Serve with dill cream.

   Dill Cream Combine ingredients in small bowl; mix well.

   MAKES 12

cheesy coriander pesto knots

2¹/₄ cups (335g) self-raising flour

2 teaspoons caster sugar

¹/₄ teaspoon salt

30g butter

1 cup (250ml) milk, approximately

100g hard goat cheese

ground black pepper

PESTO

²/₃ cup firmly packed fresh coriander leaves

¹/₂ cup (40g) coarsely grated parmesan cheese

¹/₂ cup (80g) pine nuts, toasted

1 clove garlic, crushed

2 tablespoons olive oil

1 tablespoon water

1 Sift flour, sugar and salt into medium bowl, rub in butter. Stir in enough milk to mix to a soft, sticky dough.

2 Turn dough onto floured surface, knead until smooth. Roll dough to 17cm x 30cm rectangle. Spread dough with pesto, top with crumbled cheese; sprinkle with pepper. Cut dough crossways into 3cm strips. Hold both ends of a dough strip in each hand, loop dough as if to make a knot; tuck ends under neatly. Place knots on greased oven trays about 2cm apart.

3 Bake in very hot oven about 15 minutes.

Pesto Process coriander, cheese, nuts and garlic until combined. With motor operating, gradually add oil in a thin stream; add water, process until smooth.

MAKES 10

pizza buns

2 cups (300g) self-raising
  flour
15g butter
3/4 cup (180ml) milk,
  approximately
2 teaspoons olive oil
1 tablespoon chopped fresh
  thyme
2 teaspoons packaged
  breadcrumbs

FILLING

2 teaspoons olive oil
1/2 small (40g) onion, finely
  chopped
3 bacon rashers, finely chopped
1 clove garlic, crushed
60g mushrooms, finely
  chopped
3 seeded black olives, finely
  chopped
1 tablespoon tomato paste
1 tablespoon chopped fresh
  thyme

1 Grease 20cm ring cake pan. Sift flour into medium bowl, rub in butter, stir in enough milk to mix to a soft, sticky dough.

2 Turn dough onto floured surface, knead until smooth. Divide dough into 8 pieces, knead each piece until smooth, press each piece to 10cm round, fill with a teaspoon of filling, pinch edges together to seal, shape into balls. Place balls into prepared pan. Brush with oil, sprinkle with combined thyme and breadcrumbs.

3 Bake in very hot oven 10 minutes, reduce heat to moderately hot, bake about a further 20 minutes.

Filling Heat oil in pan, add onion, bacon and garlic, cook, stirring, until bacon is crisp. Stir in mushrooms, olives, paste and thyme; cool.

MAKES 8

little crusty cheese and mustard dampers

**4 cups (600g) self-raising
  flour**
1 teaspoon dry mustard
30g butter
**2 cups (500ml) milk,
  approximately**

TOPPING

30g butter
2 tablespoons seeded mustard
1/2 teaspoon cayenne pepper
**1 1/2 cups (120g) coarsely
  grated parmesan cheese**

1 Sift flour and mustard into large bowl, rub in butter. Stir in enough milk
   to mix to a soft, sticky dough.

2 Turn dough onto floured surface, knead until smooth. Press dough out to
   about 1.5cm thickness, cut into 7cm rounds. Place rounds, just touching,
   onto greased oven trays; sprinkle with topping.

3 Bake in hot oven about 15 minutes.

   Topping Melt butter in small pan, stir in remaining ingredients.

MAKES 14

rhubarb ginger damper

15g butter

3 stems (200g) rhubarb, finely chopped

2 cups (300g) self-raising flour

pinch bicarbonate of soda

1 teaspoon ground cinnamon

$^1/_2$ cup (60g) ground almonds

2 tablespoons finely chopped crystallised ginger

$^1/_3$ cup (75g) caster sugar

1 cup (250ml) milk, approximately

2 tablespoons caster sugar, extra

1 Melt butter in small pan, add rhubarb, cook, stirring, about 5 minutes or until rhubarb is just tender; cool.

2 Sift flour, soda and cinnamon into medium bowl, stir in nuts, ginger, sugar and rhubarb. Stir in enough milk to mix to a soft, sticky dough.

3 Turn dough onto floured surface, knead until smooth. Divide dough in half, place halves onto greased oven trays, shape into 15cm rounds. Mark rounds into 8 wedges, sprinkle with extra sugar.

4 Bake in hot oven about 20 minutes.

MAKES 2

fig and apple turnover

3/4 cup (135g) roughly
chopped dried figs

1/4 cup (60ml) boiling water

2 cups (300g) self-raising
flour

1 tablespoon caster sugar

30g butter

1 cup (250ml) milk,
approximately

1 large (200g) apple, peeled,
quartered

2 teaspoons caster sugar, extra

1 Combine figs and water in small heatproof bowl, cover, stand 10 minutes. Process undrained fig mixture until smooth.

2 Sift flour and sugar into medium bowl, rub in butter. Stir in enough milk to mix to a soft, sticky dough.

3 Turn dough onto a floured surface, knead until smooth. Roll dough to 23cm x 30cm oval; spread with fig mixture. Slice apple quarters thinly with a vegetable peeler; place over half the dough lengthways, sprinkle with extra sugar. Fold dough over lengthways to cover about two-thirds of the apple. Transfer to greased oven tray; shape dough into an oval, cut diagonal slashes about 3cm apart on top of turnover, brush with a little milk.

4 Bake in very hot oven about 15 minutes. Serve dusted with icing sugar, if desired.

farmhouse spinach and double cheese plait

1 bunch (500g) English spinach

15g butter

1 medium (350g) leek, finely chopped

2 teaspoons chopped fresh thyme

2 cups (300g) self-raising flour

1 cup (80g) finely grated parmesan cheese

1 teaspoon seasoned pepper

1/4 cup chopped fresh basil leaves

3/4 cup (150g) fetta cheese, crumbled

1 cup (250ml) milk, approximately

1 Add spinach to pan of boiling water, boil 1 minute, drain, rinse under cold water; drain well. Squeeze excess moisture from spinach, chop finely.

2 Heat butter in pan, add leek and thyme, cook, stirring occasionally, until leek is soft. Add spinach, cook, stirring, about 5 minutes or until any liquid has evaporated; cool.

3 Sift flour into medium bowl, stir in parmesan, pepper, basil, three-quarters of the fetta cheese, spinach mixture and enough milk to mix to a soft, sticky dough.

4 Turn dough onto floured surface, knead until smooth. Divide dough into 3 pieces, shape into 36cm sausages. Plait sausages together on greased oven tray, sprinkle with remaining fetta cheese.

5 Bake in moderately hot oven about 40 minutes.

glossary

Almonds
BLANCHED nuts with skins removed.
FLAKED sliced nuts.
GROUND we used packaged commercially-ground nuts.
KERNELS whole nuts with skins.
SLIVERED nuts cut lengthways.
Bacon rashers also known as slices of bacon.
Baking powder a raising agent consisting mainly of 2 parts cream of tartar to 1 part bicarbonate of soda.
Beetroot also known as garden beets, red beets or, simply, beets; a hard, round sweet root vegetable.
Bicarbonate of soda also known as baking soda.
Bran flakes a packaged breakfast cereal.
Breadcrumbs
PACKAGED fine-textured, crunchy, purchased, white breadcrumbs.
STALE 1- or 2-day-old bread made into crumbs by grating, blending or processing.
Burghul also known as bulghur wheat or bulgar; hulled, steamed wheat kernels that, once dried, are crushed into various size grains.
Butter use salted or unsalted ("sweet") butter; 125g is the equivalent of 1 stick of butter.

Buttermilk a low-fat milk cultured to give a slightly sour, tangy taste; a low-fat milk can be substituted.
Butternut cookies packaged biscuits made from sugar, flour, rolled oats, butter, coconut and golden syrup.
Capsicum also known as bell pepper or, simply, pepper; red, green, yellow and deep purple varieties are available, each with a distinctive taste. Seeds and membranes should be discarded before use.
Cheese
BLUE VEIN we used a soft blue vein cheese.
FETTA a soft Greek cheese with a sharp, salty taste.
GOAT made from goat milk; both hard and soft goat cheeses are available.
GRUYERE a Swiss cheese with small holes and a nutty flavour.
PACKAGED CREAM also known as "Philly".
PARMESAN a sharp-tasting hard cheese.
RICOTTA a fresh, unripened, light curd cheese.
SMOKED we used a firm smoked cheese.
TASTY CHEDDER a mature-tasting, firm-textured cheese.
Chickpeas also known as garbanzos; irregularly round, sandy-coloured legumes.

Chocolate
CHOC BITS also known as chocolate chips; morsels of dark chocolate that hold their shape during baking.
DARK we used a good-quality cooking chocolate.
ORANGE THINS thin chocolates with orange-flavoured filling; any thin pieces of chocolate can be used.
WHITE BITS morsels of white chocolate that hold their shape during baking.
Chorizo a highly seasoned, spicy pork sausage.
Coconut use desiccated coconut unless otherwise specified.
CREAM available in cans and cartons.
FLAKED flaked, dried coconut flesh.
MILK pure, unsweetened coconut milk available in cans and cartons.
SHREDDED thin strips of dried coconut.
Cornmeal ground dried corn (maize); similar to polenta but pale yellow and finer. One can be substituted for the other, but textures will vary.
Cracked buckwheat (kasha) crushed buckwheat seeds.
Cream
FRESH (minimum fat content 35%) also known as pure cream and pouring cream; has no additives.

SOUR (minimum fat content 35%) a thick, commercially cultured soured cream.
THICKENED (minimum fat content 35%) a whipping cream containing a thickener such as gelatine.
Cucumber, Lebanese slender and thin-skinned; also known as the European or burpless cucumber.
Curry powder a combination of powdered spices consisting of chilli, coriander, cumin, fennel, fenugreek and turmeric in varying proportions.
Custard powder packaged vanilla pudding mix.
Essence an extract.
Flour
PLAIN an all-purpose flour, made from wheat.
RYE milled from rye grains.
SELF-RAISING substitute plain (all-purpose) flour and baking powder in the proportions of 1 cup (150g) plain flour to 2 level teaspoons baking powder. Sift together several times before using.
WHOLEMEAL PLAIN a whole-wheat flour without the addition of baking powder.
WHOLEMEAL SELF-RAISING a wholewheat self-raising flour; add baking powder to wholemeal plain flour as above to make wholemeal self-raising flour.

pine nuts (in bowl)
almond kernels
maple syrup
Orange Thins
golden syrup
Mars Bar
macadamias
blanched almonds
ground almonds
flaked almonds
White Bits
dark cooking chocolate
molasses
slivered almonds
Choc Bits

Ghee clarified butter; with the milk solids removed, this fat can be heated to higher temperatures than butter without burning.

Golden syrup also known as light treacle; a by-product of refined sugarcane. Pure maple syrup or honey can be substituted, but the flavour will vary.

Grand Marnier Orange-flavoured liqueur.

Jam also known as preserves or conserve; most often made from fruit.

Jersey caramel a confectionery made from sugar, glucose, condensed milk, flour, oil and gelatine.

Kibbled rye cracked rye grains.

Kumara Polynesian name of orange-fleshed sweet potato often confused with yam.

Macadamias rich and buttery nuts; store in refrigerator because of high fat content.

Maple-flavoured syrup made from cane sugar and artificial maple flavouring. Golden or pancake syrup or honey can be substituted, but the flavour will vary.

Mars Bar a confectionery bar consisting of creamy caramel and soft nougat encased in milk chocolate.

Marsala sweet fortified wine.

Milk we used full-cream homogenised milk unless otherwise specified.

SWEETENED CONDENSED we used canned milk with 60% of the water removed, and the remaining milk sweetened with sugar.

Mixed dried fruit a combination of sultanas, raisins, currants, mixed peel and cherries.

Mixed peel candied citrus peel.

Mixed spice a blend of ground spices usually consisting of cinnamon, allspice (pimento) and nutmeg.

Molasses the thick, syrupy end product of raw sugar manufacturing or refining.

Mustard

DIJON French mustard.

DRY powdered mustard seeds.

SEEDED a French-style textured mustard with crushed mustard seeds.

Nutella a chocolate hazelnut spread.

Oat bran the outer layer of oat grains.

Oil

LIGHT OLIVE a mild-flavoured olive oil.

OLIVE a blend of refined and virgin olive oils, good for everyday cooking.

VEGETABLE any of a number of oils sourced from plants rather than animal fats; we used a polyunsaturated oil.

Paprika ground dried peppers; flavour varies from mild and sweet to considerably hotter, depending on the variety of pepper.

Pastrami spicy smoked beef, ready to eat when bought.

Pepper

BLACK we used both cracked and ground black pepper.

CAYENNE also known as chilli pepper.

SEASONED a combination of black pepper, sugar and capsicum.

Pine nuts small, cream-coloured soft kernels.

Prunes whole dried plums.

Pumpkin also known as squash; a vegetable with golden flesh. Any type of pumpkin can be used.

Rhubarb a vegetable with pinkish stalks, which are generally cooked and eaten as a fruit.

Rind zest.

Rum, dark we used an underproof (not overproof) rum.

Sambal oelek (also ulek or olek) Indonesian in origin, a salty paste made from ground chillies, vinegar and various spices.

Semolina coarsely milled inner part of wheat grains.

Spinach, English a soft-leafed vegetable, more delicate in taste than silverbeet; young silverbeet can be substituted.

Stock powder we used chicken and vegetable stock powders; 1 teaspoon of stock powder is equal to 1 small stock cube.

Sugar we used coarse granulated table sugar, also known as crystal sugar, unless otherwise specified.

BROWN a soft, fine granulated sugar containing molasses.

CASTER also known as superfine; a fine granulated table sugar.

DEMERARA golden crystal sugar.

ICING also known as confectioners' sugar or powdered sugar. Icing sugar mixture contains cornflour; use pure icing sugar, if specified.

RAW natural brown granulated sugar.

Sultanas golden raisins.

Yeast allow 2 teaspoons (7g) dry yeast to each 15g compressed yeast if substituting one for the other; see also page 46 of this book for helpful information.

Zucchini also known as courgette; green, yellow or grey member of the squash family.

blue vein

parmesan

smoked

hard goat

fetta

caster sugar

demerara sugar

brown sugar

seeded mustard

dry powdered mustard

gruyere

ricotta

icing sugar mixture

Dijon mustard

conversion chart

MEASURES

One Australian metric measuring cup holds approximately 250ml, one Australian metric tablespoon holds 20ml, one Australian metric teaspoon holds 5ml.

The difference between one country's measuring cups and another's is within a two- or three-teaspoon variance, and will not affect your cooking results. North America, New Zealand and the United Kingdom use a 15ml tablespoon.

All cup and spoon measurements are level. The most accurate way of measuring dry ingredients is to weigh them. When measuring liquids, use a clear glass or plastic jug with the metric markings.

We use large eggs with an average weight of 60g.

DRY MEASURES

METRIC	IMPERIAL
15g	½oz
30g	1oz
60g	2oz
90g	3oz
125g	4oz (¼lb)
155g	5oz
185g	6oz
220g	7oz
250g	8oz (½lb)
280g	9oz
315g	10oz
345g	11oz
375g	12oz (¾lb)
410g	13oz
440g	14oz
470g	15oz
500g	16oz (1lb)
750g	24oz (1½lb)
1kg	32oz (2lb)

LIQUID MEASURES

METRIC	IMPERIAL
30ml	1 fluid oz
60ml	2 fluid oz
100ml	3 fluid oz
125ml	4 fluid oz
150ml	5 fluid oz (¼ pint/1 gill)
190ml	6 fluid oz
250ml	8 fluid oz
300ml	10 fluid oz (½ pint)
500ml	16 fluid oz
600ml	20 fluid oz (1 pint)
1000ml (1 litre)	1¾ pints

LENGTH MEASURES

METRIC	IMPERIAL
3mm	⅛in
6mm	¼in
1cm	½in
2cm	¾in
2.5cm	1in
5cm	2in
6cm	2½in
8cm	3in
10cm	4in
13cm	5in
15cm	6in
18cm	7in
20cm	8in
23cm	9in
25cm	10in
28cm	11in
30cm	12in (1ft)

OVEN TEMPERATURES

These oven temperatures are only a guide for conventional ovens. For fan-forced ovens, check the manufacturer's manual.

	°C (CELSIUS)	°F (FAHRENHEIT)	GAS MARK
Very slow	120	250	½
Slow	150	275-300	1-2
Moderately slow	160	325	3
Moderate	180	350-375	4-5
Moderately hot	200	400	6
Hot	220	425-450	7-8
Very hot	240	475	9

ARE YOU MISSING SOME OF THE WORLD'S FAVOURITE COOKBOOKS?

The Australian Women's Weekly Cookbooks are available from bookshops, cookshops, supermarkets and other stores all over the world. You can also buy direct from the publisher, using the order form below.

TITLE	RRP	QTY	TITLE	RRP	QTY
Asian, Meals in Minutes	£6.99		Indian Cooking Class	£6.99	
Babies & Toddlers Good Food	£6.99		Japanese Cooking Class	£6.99	
Barbecue Meals In Minutes	£6.99		Just For One	£6.99	
Beginners Cooking Class	£6.99		Kids' Birthday Cakes	£6.99	
Beginners Simple Meals	£6.99		Kids Cooking	£6.99	
Beginners Thai	£6.99		Kids' Cooking Step-by-Step	£6.99	
Best Food	£6.99		Lean Food	£6.99	
Best Food Desserts	£6.99		Low-carb, Low-fat	£6.99	
Best Food Fast	£6.99		Low-fat Feasts	£6.99	
Best Food Mains	£6.99		Low-fat Food For Life	£6.99	
Cafe Classics	£6.99		Low-fat Meals in Minutes	£6.99	
Cakes, Bakes & Desserts	£6.99		Main Course Salads	£6.99	
Cakes Biscuits & Slices	£6.99		Mexican	£6.99	
Cakes Cooking Class	£6.99		Middle Eastern Cooking Class	£6.99	
Caribbean Cooking	£6.99		Midweek Meals in Minutes	£6.99	
Casseroles	£6.99		Moroccan & the Foods of North Africa	£6.99	
Casseroles & Slow-Cooked Classics	£6.99		Muffins, Scones & Breads	£6.99	
Cheap Eats	£6.99		New Casseroles	£6.99	
Cheesecakes: baked and chilled	£6.99		New Classics	£6.99	
Chicken	£6.99		New Curries	£6.99	
Chicken Meals in Minutes	£6.99		New Finger Food	£6.99	
Chinese Cooking Class	£6.99		New French Food	£6.99	
Christmas Cooking	£6.99		New Salads	£6.99	
Chocolate	£6.99		Party Food and Drink	£6.99	
Cocktails	£6.99		Pasta Meals in Minutes	£6.99	
Cooking for Friends	£6.99		Potatoes	£6.99	
Cupcakes & Fairycakes	£6.99		Salads: Simple, Fast & Fresh	£6.99	
Detox	£6.99		Saucery	£6.99	
Dinner Beef	£6.99		Sauces Salsas & Dressings	£6.99	
Dinner Lamb	£6.99		Sensational Stir-Fries	£6.99	
Dinner Seafood	£6.99		Slim	£6.99	
Easy Curry	£6.99		Soup	£6.99	
Easy Spanish-Style	£6.99		Stir-fry	£6.99	
Essential Soup	£6.99		Superfoods for Exam Success	£6.99	
Foods of the Mediterranean	£6.99		Tapas Mezze Antipasto & other bites	£6.99	
Foods That Fight Back	£6.99		Thai Cooking Class	£6.99	
Fresh Food Fast	£6.99		Traditional Italian	£6.99	
Fresh Food for Babies & Toddlers	£6.99		Vegetarian Meals in Minutes	£6.99	
Good Food Fast	£6.99		Vegie Food	£6.99	
Great Lamb Cookbook	£6.99		Wicked Sweet Indulgences	£6.99	
Greek Cooking Class	£6.99		Wok, Meals in Minutes	£6.99	
Grills	£6.99				
Healthy Heart Cookbook	£6.99		TOTAL COST:	£	

Mr/Mrs/Ms _____

Address _____

_____ Postcode _____

Day time phone _____ Email* (optional) _____

I enclose my cheque/money order for £ _____

or please charge £ _____

to my: ☐ Access ☐ Mastercard ☐ Visa ☐ Diners Club

PLEASE NOTE: WE DO NOT ACCEPT SWITCH OR ELECTRON CARDS

Card number ☐☐☐☐ ☐☐☐☐ ☐☐☐☐ ☐☐☐☐

Expiry date _____ 3 digit security code *(found on reverse of card)* _____

Cardholder's name_____ Signature _____

To order: Mail or fax – photocopy or complete the order form above, and send your credit card details or cheque payable to: Australian Consolidated Press (UK), Moulton Park Business Centre, Red House Road, Moulton Park, Northampton NN3 6AQ, phone (+44) (0) 1604 497531 fax (+44) (0) 1604 497533, e-mail books@acpuk.com or order online at www.acpuk.com

Non-UK residents: We accept the credit cards listed on the coupon, or cheques, drafts or International Money Orders payable in sterling and drawn on a UK bank. Credit card charges are at the exchange rate current at the time of payment.

Postage and packing UK: Add £1.00 per order plus 50p per book.

Postage and packing overseas: Add £2.00 per order plus £1.00 per book.

All pricing current at time of going to press and subject to change/availability.

Offer ends 31.12.2007

* By including your email address, you consent to receipt of any email regarding this magazine, and other emails which inform you of ACP's other publications, products, services and events, and to promote third party goods and services you may be interested in.